Early Home Learning Matters
A good practice guide

Kim Roberts

The Family and Parenting Institute researches what matters to families and parents. We use our knowledge to influence policymakers and foster public debate. We develop ideas to improve the services families use and the environment in which children grow up.

Family and Parenting Institute
430 Highgate Studios
53–79 Highgate Road
London NW5 1TL

Tel 020 7424 3460
Fax 020 7485 3590
Email info@familyandparenting.org
Websites www.familyandparenting.org
www.earlyhomelearning.org.uk

ISBN 978-1-903615-77-5

Registered charity number: 1077444
Registered company number: 3753345
VAT registration number: 833024365

The Family and Parenting Institute is the operating name of the National Family and Parenting Institute (NFPI). NFPI is a company limited by guarantee, registered in England and Wales.

Contents

Acknowledgements

This guide has been funded by the Department for Children, Schools and Families (DCSF). The Family and Parenting Institute (FPI) gratefully acknowledges their support.

Thank you to everyone who helped with the content and design of this book, particularly to the many parents and practitioners who shared their stories, information and learning as part of the Early Learning Partnerships Project (ELPP) and Parents as Partners in Early Learning (PPEL) project.

I am also grateful to:

Jenny Reynolds and Daphne Cotton for research advice and information. Some of the data and content in this book draws on their joint study of local authority early learning services *Supporting the early home learning environment: messages from research with local authorities and insights from literature* (2009), and Jenny's unpublished literature review *Supporting the early home learning environment: a review of the literature* (2009).

Ruth Corney for the photographs that bring the book to life.

Staff at Coram; families at Coram for agreeing to be photographed; Parents, Early Years and Learning (PEAL); Campaign for Learning (CfL); and Parents as First Teachers for generously making the time to talk about work with parents, and sharing practice examples and resources.

Salia Nessa for coordinating editing, design and production.

Allan Watson for being an unfailingly supportive sounding board and providing well-informed feedback throughout the writing process.

Finally, to my three daughters, Cora, Ellie and Tess, from whom I have learned so much about parenting.

Kim Roberts
April 2009

Foreword

The evidence for making early years support an essential part of a child's development is now incontrovertible. We know that action in the early years represents our biggest chance to sever the link between disadvantage and low achievement. Research tells us that by the age of 22 months the learning development of children from disadvantaged backgrounds can start to slip back behind that of other children from more advantaged backgrounds. We know that the home learning environment is the single biggest influence on a child's development. If we want to give every child the best possible start in life, in every setting, all our services must be delivered in partnership with parents – mothers and fathers.

This book sets out clearly how people working in the early years and those commissioning early years services can support mothers and fathers to offer their child the best possible start in life. There isn't a one-size-fits-all solution. It's all about relationships, and we're all very different. This guide sets out clearly how children develop, and shows the kind of interactions that make a big difference, to children, to parents, and to practitioners.

In a lot of cases, mothers and fathers want help, but help of a particular kind. They need practical ideas, advice and confidence to do the right things at the right time. Often it's simple things – getting parents to sing nursery rhymes with the children, read with them, play with letters and numbers – that have the biggest effect. Many don't realise this kind of play and communication can make such a difference.

My ambition is to ensure the support mothers and fathers want is there where – and when – they need it, without judgement, without prejudice. Evidence shows that most parents, including the most vulnerable and those whom services find it hardest to engage, want the best for their children. And it builds up a virtuous circle – parents getting this kind of support gain confidence in their abilities, greater appreciation for the skills of the professionals involved, and fresh ideas for playing and talking with their children. But, perhaps more importantly, they also often find their relationship with the child improves – more cuddles, more showing of affection, more attachment and frankly, in many cases, more fun.

This is an exciting time for the sector – a time of real growth and big opportunity. In September 2008, we launched the Early Years Foundation Stage, which has at its heart the relationship between providers and parents. In January 2009, we published *Next Steps for Early Learning and Childcare: Building on the 10-Year Strategy*, alongside the Child Poverty Bill. This set out our continued commitment to promote child development, supporting employment and recognising families' preferences, and included a comprehensive assessment on parental leave policies, an expansion of Every Child a Talker in the most disadvantaged areas, a new childcare price comparison website for parents, piloting raising the tax credit limit for families in London and those with disabled children as part of the Childcare Affordability Pilot.

There's also the entitlement to free nursery care, which we have pledged to expand to 15 hours for every three- and four-year-old by 2010, and increasing the offer more flexibly to meet parents' needs. And by 2010, there will be a Sure Start Children's Centre for every community – already we have over 3,000 up and running.

So, against this background of continuing development and activity in the early years sector, I commend this book as essential reading for all those working to support the best possible outcomes for children.

Dawn Primarolo
Minister of State for Children, Young People and Families

Introduction

What is this book about?

This book is about supporting parents, fathers as well as mothers, to provide the kind of relationships and experiences at home that very young children need in order to flourish – while enjoying family life and time together.

Early home learning is everything that children from birth to age five do or experience with their parents that positively influences their learning, development and later achievement – from security and warm, loving attention, to playing, talking, singing and looking at books together.

The word 'parent' is used throughout to include anyone involved in bringing up children, including mothers, fathers, male and female carers, grandparents, step-parents, and other family members.

Why has the book been written?

The evidence is overwhelming. Parental involvement in early learning as part of daily family life at home has a greater impact on children's wellbeing and achievement than any other factor, such as poverty, parental education or school environment. Supporting parents to provide a positive home learning environment is therefore a vital part of improving outcomes for children, particularly those from disadvantaged backgrounds.

The important role played by parents is recognised in the Early Years Foundation Stage (EYFS), which explicitly includes work with parents as partners in their children's early learning and services to support early learning at home.

Early Home Learning Matters: A good practice guide has been written to support good practice for all those working with parents of very young children, to involve them in early learning, as well as those involved in planning early years services.

It arises from the work of two demonstration projects funded by the Department for Children, Schools and Families (DCSF): Early Learning Partnerships Project (ELPP) and Parents as Partners in Early Learning (PPEL). These projects involved many local authorities and voluntary sector organisations working together between 2006 and 2008 to develop innovative and joined-up approaches to work with parents in order to engage them in their young children's early learning. The good practice generated by both projects is used in this book to provide a framework for services and settings seeking to develop or extend their activities to support early home learning.

Who is this book for?

Early Home Learning Matters: A good practice guide is a resource for all early years practitioners and those involved in planning and implementing services for parents of children from birth to age five.

This book is for practitioners who want to extend their knowledge and confidence in working with parents of young children as partners, and brings together what you need to know to successfully involve vulnerable parents in their children's early learning. Chapters 5 and 6 provide lots of examples from practice, and ideas to help you reach and engage parents with different needs, including fathers, families from minority ethnic backgrounds and parents with additional support needs.

Early Home Learning Matters: A good practice guide is also highly relevant for managers, service leads and commissioners. ELPP and PPEL highlighted the need to embed knowledge and understanding about the importance of parental involvement in early learning at strategic level.

This book provides essential information for anyone seeking to develop early years services and strengthen support for early learning at home as a key part of improving outcomes for children.

How will this book help?

It will help you:

- understand why working in partnership with parents is so vital in improving children's achievement and wellbeing
- think through the key issues in developing effective services
- make decisions about who you are trying to reach
- reflect on your current practice
- reach and engage diverse and vulnerable families
- decide what services and activities will help you to involve fathers, families from minority ethnic backgrounds and parents with additional support needs

- ensure you have a properly trained and supervised workforce to deliver the work
- measure and demonstrate the impact of your work on outcomes for children.

Early Home Learning Matters: A good practice guide combines messages from policy and research with examples from practice, parents' experiences and information about resources that are available to support you in your work with parents. It is designed to be used as a practical resource to support people with differing roles. Each chapter starts with a summary of its contents so that you can select the information most relevant to you and/or your setting.

An accompanying website – **www.earlyhomelearning.org.uk** – contains a parents' section with resources that you can download to share with parents.

Chapter 1
Why work with parents?

This chapter brings together the overwhelming research evidence about the importance of work with parents – fathers as well as mothers – in the early years in order to improve outcomes for children, particularly those from disadvantaged backgrounds. How parents relate to, and engage with, their young children from birth to five can dramatically affect their children's later learning and achievement.

This information is vital, whether you are working directly with families with very young children or thinking about how this knowledge from research can be applied to develop services that will change life trajectories for disadvantaged children.

The policy framework and the Early Years Foundation Stage (EYFS) underpinning work with parents in the early years is summarised; this provides the wider context and background to the development of services to support early learning in the home.

Bucking the trend: improving outcomes for children from disadvantaged backgrounds

We know that poverty and social disadvantage are key factors linked to poor outcomes for children. However, research clearly shows that the link between deprivation and underachievement is not set in stone. The Effective Provision of Pre-School Education (EPPE) study (Sylva et al., 2004) found that the quality of the early home learning environment is an even stronger predictor of achievement than material circumstances.

Early home learning is not just about the kind of pre-educational activities that the words may suggest. It encompasses a much wider range of experiences that provide the foundation from which babies and young children can grow to achieve their full potential. How parents, mothers and fathers, relate to their children from the moment of birth and the activities they do with them inside and outside the home during their early years have a major impact on children's later social, emotional and intellectual development.

The evidence is unequivocal: when parents have the knowledge, skills and confidence to provide the kind of relationships and experiences that children need in the early years, it makes a real difference to children's futures.

Is it possible to change what parents do?

Yes.

The Oxford evaluation of the Early Learning Partnerships Project (ELPP) (Evangelou et al., 2008) found that:

- it is possible to engage parents from every background in their children's learning

- it is possible to improve the home learning environment.

The Parents as Partners in Early Learning (PPEL) project (DCSF, 2008) found that the vast majority of parents were keen to help their children, but sometimes needed support to do so. When this support was offered, it had a significant impact, with promising outcomes for:

- children's development and learning

- parents' confidence and knowledge about what's best for their children

- the parent–child relationship.

The National Evaluation of Sure Start (NESS) points to similar conclusions about the positive impact of parental involvement in children's early learning. It found that families living within Sure Start Local Programme (SSLP) areas showed less negative parenting and provided children with a better home learning environment than families in similar areas that did not have an SSLP.

NESS concluded that these beneficial parenting effects appeared to be responsible for the higher level of positive social behaviour in children in SSLP areas. Three-year-olds in SSLP areas showed better social development, exhibiting more positive social behaviour and greater independence and self-regulation than their non-SSLP counterparts.

Key messages from research

Parenting behaviour influences children's development from the moment of birth
(Gutman and Feinstein 2007; Feinstein, 2003)

- The link between disadvantage and achievement is evident from an early age. More able children from deprived backgrounds are predicted to fall behind less able children from less deprived backgrounds from as early as 22 months.

- The mother's level of education has a particularly marked effect on parental involvement in early learning and child development.

- In home environments where mothers provided more stimulation and teaching, child development on all measures was generally higher, regardless of the mother's level of education or economic circumstances.

Fathers have an important role to play
(Flouri and Buchanan, 2001; Hobcraft, 1998)

- Children whose fathers are involved in their learning do better at school and have better mental health, even after other factors such as fathers' socio-economic status and education have been taken out of the equation.

- Fathers' lack of interest in schooling is a particularly strong predictor of lack of qualifications.

The influence of the home is 'enduring, pervasive and direct'
(Desforges, 2003)

- What parents do at home has a significant positive effect on children's achievement and adjustment even after all other factors have been taken out of the equation.

- Children not only gain skills at home, but also absorb a positive attitude to and enthusiasm for learning.

- Parental involvement has a positive impact across all ethnic groups and social classes.

- In the primary age range, parental involvement has a greater impact on achievement than the quality of schools.

Continued

Continued

What parents do is more important than who they are
(Sylva et al., 2004)

- For all children, the quality of the home learning environment is more important for intellectual and social development than parental occupation, education or income.

- Parents' involvement in their children's early learning at home has continued and significant positive benefits on attainment and social behaviour at ages 7, 10 and 11.

- Children whose parents regularly engage in home learning activities were less likely to be assessed for special educational needs.

- The quality of the home learning environment provided by families from some minority ethnic groups has an even stronger impact on children's achievement than would be expected given their socio-economic status and other background characteristics.

- Fewer boys than girls are engaged by their parents in play and early learning activities in the home.

It is possible to engage vulnerable parents and improve the home learning environment
(Evangelou et al., 2008)

- Parents participating in early learning services with their children demonstrated significant improvements in their awareness of their children's needs and ability to provide learning opportunities.

- Parental involvement in early learning was linked to positive changes in parenting, including spending more time with their children and demonstrating more emotional warmth, and positive changes in children's attachment, behaviour and development.

Implications for early years services

The DCSF briefing for local authorities *Supporting parents to engage in their child's early learning* (DCSF, 2008) highlights the evidence from ELPP in showing why programmes and mainstream funding that support parental engagement in their young children's learning and development should be prioritised within local decision making, and Children and Young People's Plans.

The research evidence about the importance of a child's early years is highly significant when making strategic decisions about allocation of resources. A child's future is significantly shaped by early relationships, brain development and learning opportunities. The earlier in a child's life that resources to support parenting and parent involvement in learning are focused, the more impact they will have in turning round cycles of disadvantage.

Early years services can help young children to achieve their potential by:

● supporting fathers' and mothers' bonding with and attachment to their young children

● helping to stimulate the home learning environment by encouraging parents to engage in play and simple learning activities at home

● working with parents to stimulate their involvement in and access to early years education.

Policy framework

"Government does not bring up children – parents do – so Government needs to do more to back parents and families."
(DCSF, 2007)

The vital role of parents, both fathers and mothers, in early learning to secure good outcomes for children is reflected in the Government's policy agenda for children, young people and their families.

Work with parents in the early years forms part of the EYFS, which came into force in September 2008. The EYFS provides the regulatory and quality framework for the provision of learning, development and care for children between birth and the academic year in which they turn five (0–5).

Figure 1.1 Development of Government policy relevant to parents of early years children

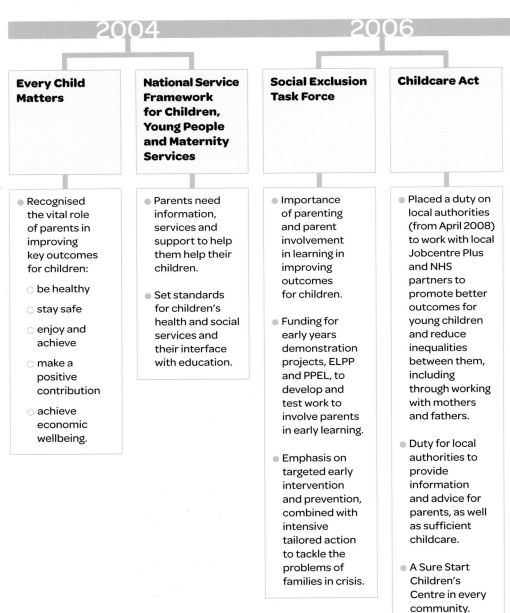

2004

2006

Every Child Matters

National Service Framework for Children, Young People and Maternity Services

Social Exclusion Task Force

Childcare Act

- Recognised the vital role of parents in improving key outcomes for children:
  - be healthy
  - stay safe
  - enjoy and achieve
  - make a positive contribution
  - achieve economic wellbeing.

- Parents need information, services and support to help them help their children.

- Set standards for children's health and social services and their interface with education.

- Importance of parenting and parent involvement in learning in improving outcomes for children.

- Funding for early years demonstration projects, ELPP and PPEL, to develop and test work to involve parents in early learning.

- Emphasis on targeted early intervention and prevention, combined with intensive tailored action to tackle the problems of families in crisis.

- Placed a duty on local authorities (from April 2008) to work with local Jobcentre Plus and NHS partners to promote better outcomes for young children and reduce inequalities between them, including through working with mothers and fathers.

- Duty for local authorities to provide information and advice for parents, as well as sufficient childcare.

- A Sure Start Children's Centre in every community.

2007   2008   2009

Children's Plan

- Prevention to avoid failure.

- Commitment that by 2020 every child will be 'ready for success in school', with at least 90 per cent developing well across all areas of the EYFS by age five.

- Involvement of parents through a partnership approach and parent councils.

Every Parent Matters

- Brings together the ways in which Government is promoting increased parental involvement and confidence, as well as parents' involvement in shaping services for themselves and their children.

- Importance of fathers' involvement in outcomes for children.

- Parent Know-How to provide information for parents about parenting issues and how to support their children's learning.

Early Years Foundation Stage

- Integrates education and care for all 0–5 children accessing early education and childcare through a personalised, play-based approach.

- Parents are children's first and most enduring educators.

- Children learn to be strong and independent from a base of love and secure relationships.

- Parents and practitioners working in partnership have a positive impact on children's development and learning.

Next Steps for Early Learning and Childcare

- Needs of friends and relatives who care for children to be taken into account.

- New research to understand the skills/behaviours of effective providers in working with parents.

- Workforce development for early years services.

Chapter 2
What is a good home learning environment?

In this chapter . . .

This chapter summarises some of the key messages about early development and the ways that parents can provide the quality of nurturing, play and learning activities at home that provide the building blocks for children's learning and achievement.

This information will give you an understanding of what parents can do to support their children's early learning as a natural part of daily family life at home. Understanding the key elements of a positive home learning environment will help you to develop effective practice and services – and communicate clear messages to mothers and fathers.

Barnet and Barnet (1998) describe development as "a lifelong dialogue between inherited tendencies and our life history".

The home is the single most significant environmental factor in enabling children to develop the trust, attitude and skills that will help them to learn and engage positively with the world. A good home learning environment provides the love, security, stimulation, encouragement and opportunities that help children to flourish – a process that starts at birth, if not before.

The building blocks for learning: early brain development

In the last 25 years, technological advances have enabled important new discoveries about the growth of the human brain and the impact of a young child's experiences on their development.

The human brain is unfinished at birth. A baby's brain develops at an astonishing pace; it develops from 25 per cent of the fully formed brain at birth to 80 per cent by the age of three.

This development is 'experience dependent'. A baby is born with most, if not all, of their brain cells in place. After birth, however, connections (synapses) are developed that pass information between the brain's nerve cells. Imagine a new house with all the wiring in place, but not yet connected; the electricity will only work once the circuits have been connected.

The patterns of connection that form between the brain's nerve cells govern the development of language and emotion, as well as cognitive, physical and sensory abilities. The more an experience (positive or negative) is repeated, the stronger the connection.

After a period of rapid growth from birth to age three, when the brain makes trillions of new connections, some of these connections are 'pruned' away. Connections that have been repeatedly used grow stronger, start to form well-trodden pathways and are retained, while those that have not been used often are shed. This results literally in a smaller, less developed brain with fewer connections across which messages can be passed between nerve cells. The difference between the brain of a 'normally developed' three-year-old and the brain of a three-year-old who has experienced sensory deprivation is graphically illustrated in the pictures below.

Figure 2.1 Abnormal brain development following sensory neglect in early childhood (Perry, 2005)

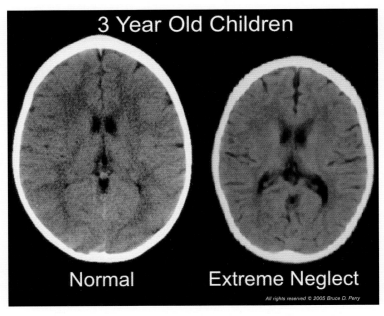

These images illustrate the negative impact of neglect on the developing brain. The CT scan on the left is from a healthy three-year-old child with an average head size (50th percentile). The image on the right is from a three-year-old child following severe sensory deprivation neglect since birth. The brain is significantly smaller than average and has abnormal development of cortical, limbic and midbrain structures.

From studies conducted by researchers from The ChildTrauma Academy (www.ChildTrauma.org) led by Bruce D. Perry, M.D., Ph.D.

The importance of relationship for the developing brain

The quality of the relationship between parent and child during the first three years is fundamental to children's longer-term development (O'Connor and Scott, 2007). When parents provide warm, loving attention, this builds the baby's future capacity for empathy and self-control, both of which have a major impact on later life. A child who finds it difficult to focus, control their behaviour and relate to their peers and teaching staff is more likely to become trapped in an escalating cycle of school disaffection.

Schore (1994) describes how the relationship between baby and adult carer affects the physical development of the part of the brain that governs the capacity for empathy and self-control (the orbitofrontal cortex), which grows almost entirely after birth in response to social experiences.

Experiences can also damage the developing brain

The baby's brain does not only develop (or not) in response to positive interaction. New research contains important messages about the damaging impact of stress and the stress hormone, cortisol, on the developing brain.

Babies are not able to manage their own stress and need to have stressful experiences managed for them. They have low levels of cortisol for the first few months as long as adult carers maintain their equilibrium by soothing them when necessary.

A baby whose stress is not kept at a manageable level may eventually be seriously affected. Lyons et al. (2000) suggest that high levels of cortisol can be toxic, damaging the brain and adversely affecting later emotional life.

Windows of opportunity for the developing brain

The rapid development of the human brain during the first three years of life provides what are often described as 'windows of opportunity' for the development of vision, hearing, language, emotions and motor skills. While there is some disagreement in the literature about the extent to which the brain's plasticity allows individuals to make up physical and psychological losses after early deprivation, there is widespread agreement about the critical periods for optimum development.

Table 2.1 **Windows of opportunity for the developing brain**

Brain development	Critical period of time
Vision	Birth to two years
Hearing	Six months to one year
Language	Birth to six years
Emotions	Birth to three years
Motor skills	Throughout childhood

Attachment and the developing child

Attachment research highlights the fact that sensitive and loving caregiving, and the development of a secure relationship with one or more loving carers, are central to optimal child development.

The roots of attachment theory can be traced to the work of British psychiatrist, John Bowlby, who believed that:

" . . . the propensity to make strong emotional bonds to particular individuals [is] a basic component of human nature." (1988)

Bowlby's colleague, Mary Ainsworth, empirically tested these ideas by observing mothers and infants interacting in their homes during the infant's first year. From these studies, Ainsworth observed that the mothers who responded to their infants' need for attention sensitively and appropriately were more likely to have infants who cried little and were content to explore their environment in their mother's presence. She concluded that these infants were 'securely' attached, and that this security was supported by warm and sensitive parenting behaviours.

Findings consistently suggest that a secure attachment status is related to greater self-confidence, improved social skills and higher school achievement (Sroufe et al., 2005).

Translating knowledge into action

Birth to toddlerhood: what do babies need to build a foundation for learning?

The evidence that parenting behaviour can positively or adversely affect babies' development is overwhelming. So what are the most important things parents can provide during babyhood to promote positive brain development?

Figure 2.2 Activities that promote babies' development

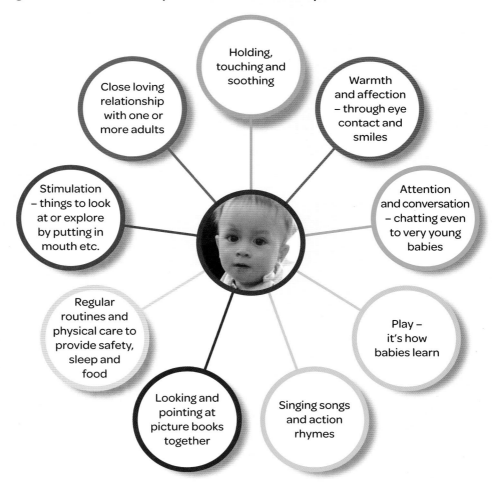

From toddlerhood to starting school: what can parents do to promote their young child's early learning?

Studies examining a good home learning environment for young children as they move beyond babyhood have focused on the activities that parents, fathers and mothers, undertake and the opportunities they provide for their children to promote the development of a positive attitude to learning, as well as the acquisition of motor, intellectual, social and emotional skills.

Desforges (2003) defined 'at home good parenting' as providing:

- a secure and stable environment
- intellectual stimulation
- parent–child discussion
- high aspirations.

The EPPE study (Sylva et al., 2004) used the Home Observation for Measurement of the Environment (HOME) scale to score the home learning environment in terms of:

- responsivity
- acceptance
- organisation
- learning materials
- involvement in learning
- variety.

The EPPE study, with other research, found that the following activities (Figure 2.3), had a marked impact on children's learning.

Figure 2.3 Activities that promote young children's development

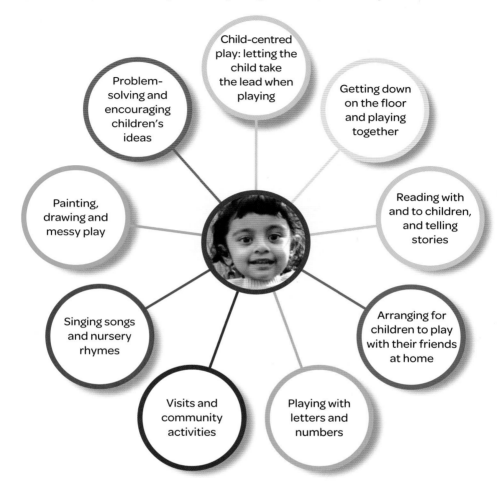

The importance of talking to young children

Hart and Risley's (1995) long-term study highlighted the direct connection between talking to children and children's linguistic and intellectual development. The study involved 42 families who were classified into three main groups:

- professional families
- working-class families
- families who were on welfare support.

By recording and analysing the verbal interactions between parents and their children from the age of about 10 months to three years, they established progressive differences in the language abilities of the children from the three types of home background.

Although children from all of the groups started to speak at about the same time and also developed good structure and use of language, their vocabulary, as measured by the number of different words used, varied significantly and correlated directly to the number of words they had heard spoken, illustrated in Table 2.2 below.

Table 2.2 Correlation between language development and the number of words children hear spoken

Home background	Number of words children heard per hour	Child's cumulative vocabulary
Professional families	2,153	1,100
Working-class families	1,253	750
Families on welfare benefits	616	500

Does it matter how parents talk to their children?

Hart and Risley (1995) also identified the kind of talking that benefited children's development and that could be applied to all of the families.

Five specific ways that parents talked to children consistently had the most positive impact:

- **They just talked**, generally using a wide vocabulary as part of daily life.

- **They tried to be nice**, expressing praise and acceptance and few negative commands.

- **They told children about things**, using language with a high information content.

- **They gave children choices**, asking them their opinion rather than simply telling them what to do.

- **They listened**, responding to them rather than ignoring what they said or making demands.

These ways of talking to and interacting with children had a strong relationship with children's IQ scores at age 3. When a group of 29 of the children were followed up at ages 9 to 10, the difference in verbal ability was still evident in 61 per cent of the children.

Bringing it all together

"Home-based play activities are best delivered in the context of warm, loving relationships that build a child's self-esteem."
(Wheeler and Connor, 2009)

Sylva et al. (2004) identified particular activities that 'stretch a child's mind':

- reading with and to children
- singing songs and rhymes
- going on visits
- painting and drawing
- creating opportunities to play with friends
- going to the library
- playing with letters and numbers.

Example from practice

 The **Dove Children's Centre in Wolverhampton** has developed activity boxes that parents can share with their children at home, involving parents in the design and contents of the boxes. Each box has a focus, such as healthy eating or musical instruments. The boxes come complete with directions for use and a notebook, so that parents and practitioners can exchange comments about children's learning. Families can borrow a box for up to two weeks.

The boxes help to promote the importance of parents playing and interacting with their children as part of everyday life. Parents have shared ideas with each other, talked more about what their children enjoy doing and informed practitioners of what they do at home to extend learning. The activity boxes have also given parents more insight into what play activities are possible at home and just how much children learn through enjoyable play.

Source: Wheeler and Connor (2009)

Chapter 3
Engaging parents

In this chapter . . .

Whether you're developing services or working directly with parents, this chapter will help you identify which families you need to reach in order to make the most impact on outcomes for children.

It will also explore what stops some parents accessing support and how services can manage the tension between universal and targeted provision in overcoming these barriers.

For those providing services, there are practice examples and information about how to effectively engage vulnerable families, with a checklist to enable you to review your current practice and how you could make your service more inclusive.

Who are you trying to reach?

In Chapter 1 the widely established link between social disadvantage and poor outcomes for children was discussed. This information is crucial in enabling services to reach and engage those families whose children are most at risk of underachievement.

Extensive research has looked more closely at specific key predictors of learning delay within the broad spectrum of 'social disadvantage' (C4EO, 2009; Harvard Family Research Project, 2006; Sidebotham et al., 2002; Bradley et al., 2001; Snow et al., 1998). The following factors have been consistently identified by the different studies:

- poverty – which affects certain ethnic groups disproportionately
- health issues, such as illness and disability
- mother's educational background
- low parental aspirations and disinterest in education
- parents with limited English or literacy
- family instability

- poor early care and socialisation
- lack of bonding and attachment to parents
- controlling, critical and harsh parenting.

What is meant by 'learning delay'?

The term 'learning delay' can be used broadly to describe children who are falling behind in terms of intellectual, emotional and personal development. The words 'learning delay' are not used here as a clinical diagnosis or assessment of special educational needs.

The evidence of this learning delay can be identified from an early age. Feinstein (2003) used simple tasks with 22-month-old babies and found significant differences between the average children in the top and bottom social class groups.

More specifically, within early learning studies, the term 'learning delay' has been used to describe lack of school readiness (Olds, 2006; Snow et al., 1998) – children who are less likely to start school prepared for formal education and learning.

Targeted services versus universal provision

Many elements of services to support early home learning are universal, such as health visiting, information about child development, and local activities and facilities aimed at parents and young children.

Given that resources are limited, however, clear decisions about priorities for more intensive support and services need to be made. Services will need to target and engage high-risk families before children start to fall behind, if they are to succeed in their aim of preventing learning delay.

The research evidence that the occurrence of learning delay is found within similar types of families is important here and enables services to be guided by criteria of disadvantage rather than specific diagnosis of learning delay when making these decisions.

This approach to effective targeting of resources depends, however, on a sound knowledge of the local community. This knowledge can be built from different sources, including:

- strategic multi-agency audits of local needs to identify families in which children are at high risk of learning delay
- monitoring of service uptake by these families

- personal knowledge of the local area gained from talking to parents or practitioners who live locally

- working in partnership with grass-roots community groups.

Targeting services in this way can be helpful in making the most effective use of resources and reaching families most in need of support. Moving beyond universal provision does, however, run the risk of alienating the very families services are trying to reach. Targeting needs to be done in a way that is empowering, valuing and avoids creating stigma by labelling 'problem families', if it is to achieve its aim of engaging the parents of children at risk of learning delay.

Targeting services within identified geographical areas of deprivation can therefore be an important factor in reaching families who most need support, but it is not on its own sufficient. For instance, initially it was found that some of the most disadvantaged families in Sure Start Local Programme areas, such as teenage parents, workless households and lone parents, did not make use of the services available (Anning et al., 2007). Subsequently, better outreach and home visiting services in Sure Start Children's Centres have helped to remedy this. Large-scale early years demonstration projects, including the ELPP 2006–08 and PPEL 2006–08, have demonstrated the need to target both geographical areas of disadvantage and vulnerable families within these areas. Vulnerable families within this context can be defined as those with one or more of the key predictors of learning delay listed above.

What prevents parental involvement?

Parents lack knowledge not interest

"We need to begin with the firm belief that all parents are interested in the development and progress of their own children."
Pen Green Centre for Under Fives and Families

To practitioners grappling with the challenges of engaging parents, it can sometimes seem that parents just aren't bothered. It's not surprising that practitioners form this opinion after discouraging and repeated experiences of parents being out when they call for arranged home visits or not turning up to group sessions after saying they would come.

The reality, however, is much more complex and challenges these assumptions. Both experience from practice and findings from research conclude that lack of interest is not one of the major factors standing in the way of parental involvement in learning:

- at Pen Green Centre for Under Fives and Families, 84 per cent of parents sustained their role in supporting their child's learning when offered a flexible range of options for involvement (Whalley, 2001)

- one recent large survey found that two-thirds of parents would like to be more involved in their children's education and the desire to get more involved tended to be stronger among disadvantaged groups (Peters et al., 2007)

- the ELPP and PPEL project showed that it is possible to engage vulnerable parents in their children's learning.

It seems that some parents, fathers and mothers, lack knowledge, information and resources, but not interest. So what are the factors that get in the way and prevent parents from getting the support and knowledge that they need, and that services can provide?

Barriers to parental involvement

Research has identified a range of barriers to parental involvement in children's early learning (Wheeler and Connor, 2009). Some of these barriers are to do with how the service is provided and parents' experiences of using services. Others relate to individual parents and their circumstances.

Barriers at the service/practitioner level

- Poor communication on the part of practitioners, such as using jargon and behaving like the expert when talking to parents.

- Lack of practitioner knowledge about the importance of parental involvement.

- Lack of practitioner confidence and skills to work with parents.

- Services not tailored to parents' needs, level of knowledge or circumstances.

- Practitioner resistance to parental involvement.

- Negative attitudes towards parents and a lack of respect for, and recognition of, their role.

- Location of settings and inadequate transport.

- Unwelcoming venues and lack of space.

- Staff unrepresentative of the parents they are trying to reach, for example low numbers of male role models in the workforce is a barrier to engaging fathers.

- Lack of funding and capacity.

Barriers at the parent level

Experiences and beliefs

- Poor experiences of school or professionals, leading to negative attitudes and lack of trust on the part of parents.

- Fear of being judged as a failing parent.

- Past and ongoing experience of discrimination.

- Low value placed on education.

- Beliefs about keeping children at home until they are old enough to start school.

Life factors

- Work pressures and working long hours or unpredictable work patterns.

- Inflexible timing of services.

- Lack of childcare.

- Stressful lives and circumstances, for example poverty, mental health, single parenthood, disability, illness, family transience.

Knowledge

- Not understanding the difference they can make to their child's development.

- Lack of confidence and knowledge about how to be involved.

- Inappropriate expectations of children's development.

- Lack of knowledge about local services or opportunities.

- Parents' own literacy and numeracy levels are poor.

- Lack of confidence in English if it is not their first language.

So how can early years services involve parents?

In their extensive study of what works in parenting support, Moran et al. (2004) looked at what helped services in:

- **'getting'** parents (enabling them to use the service in the first place)

- **'keeping'** parents (enabling them to attend sessions regularly or complete a course)

- **'engaging'** parents (making it possible for them to engage actively in what the service has to offer).

They highlighted the importance of five factors in successfully managing these tasks:

- relational
- practical
- cultural
- contextual
- strategic and structural.

The importance of relationships and partnership

"Recognising parents' expertise in their own children and lives, doing things with families rather than to them is crucial."
Moran et al. (2004)

We know that parents want to remain in control of their family lives, be listened to and be treated as active participants in meeting children's needs (Quinton, 2004).

Relationships are at the heart of this process. For a parent lacking the confidence and trust to access services, forming a warm and positive relationship with a practitioner can be the bridge to available help and information.

Parents, both fathers and mothers, give consistent and clear messages about the kind of relationship with and help from professionals that are effective for them. They want to:

- remain in control of their family lives and be treated as active participants in meeting children's needs
- be listened to and treated with respect
- be helped by 'professional friends' – practitioners who are confident and well-informed, but who are also able to get alongside parents and show an interest in them and their lives
- have clear information and advice about their children's needs and how they can meet them
- have practical guidance to build their confidence and skills in providing positive early learning experiences
- join in activities with their child where they can meet other parents, have fun and share experiences.

While work with parents plays such a vital role in early years services, many early learning projects are staffed by practitioners whose primary expertise is in work with children and who may feel de-skilled when working with parents. Recognising the importance of core relationship skills can, however, help practitioners to feel more confident in using skills and qualities they already have.

Braun et al. (2006) explored the tasks involved in the helping process and identified the qualities that enable practitioners to build effective relationships and partnerships with parents. Consideration of these qualities can inform recruitment decisions, as well as be incorporated in supervision and training for practitioners.

The qualities that underpin a helping relationship and partnership

- **Respect:** valuing parents as individuals, believing in their fundamental ability to cope and make a difference in their family lives, and working within an ethos of partnership.

- **Empathy:** showing an understanding of the challenges a parent is facing in their lives and being able to see the situation from their point of view.

- **Genuineness:** being sensitive, honest, undefensive and trustworthy.

- **Humility:** working in the context of an equal relationship and using parents' strengths, views and knowledge alongside your own at every stage of the process.

- **Quiet enthusiasm:** bringing a friendly, positive energy to the relationship and a consistently calm, steady and warm approach.

- **Personal integrity:** in addition to empathising with the parent, being able to hold alternative views and offer these when appropriate.

- **Expertise:** the knowledge and experience that the helper brings to the work to complement the parent's existing knowledge and skills, both in building the relationship and in providing information and support.

(Braun et al., 2006)

Overcoming barriers to involvement

Settings and services tend to build up a momentum over time that leads to services being delivered in certain ways because 'that's how it's always been done'.

Tailoring services to meet the needs of specific groups is about recognising what prevents parents' involvement, and understanding the need for flexibility and responsiveness in the light of parents' varying needs, lifestyles and cultures.

ELPP showed that it is possible to reach and engage vulnerable families in disadvantaged areas in educationally oriented initiatives. The project's evaluators echoed Moran et al.'s (2004) conclusions about what works in encouraging parent participation and retention, highlighting the importance of:

- consulting parents about service design and activities
- 'diversifying' the nature of the support provided, for instance setting-based services added home visiting to their menu of support and vice versa
- maintaining a focus on the needs of vulnerable families
- adapting provision to fit parents' needs.

A major shift in focus for many services that participated in the ELPP and PPEL projects was to see vulnerable adults primarily as parents rather than clients and to bring them into a partnership that recognised the importance of their involvement in their child's learning.

Key messages

- Allow enough time for focused and persistent outreach to ensure vulnerable families within targeted areas of need are included.
- Develop practitioner capacity and expertise in relation to outreach work.
- 'Take the service to the parent' where necessary, rather than wait for parents to come to settings. Work with parents in the home has a particularly important role in reaching and engaging the most vulnerable parents.
- Provide services in flexible ways and at flexible times.
- Tailor activities to make them appealing to parents who make less use of early years provision, for instance fathers.
- Involving parents in early home learning activities can provide a way of reaching vulnerable parents who would not otherwise access services. The focus on helping their children learn, rather than on generic parenting skills, can lessen the feelings of inadequacy that may prevent parents seeking help.
- Services to engage the most vulnerable families in their children's early home learning can't stand alone. They need to be part of a raft of services to address multiple needs.
- A flexible approach is needed when helping vulnerable adults to engage in their child's early home learning, with practitioners making informed, responsive decisions about how to best support and involve the parent. Other issues, such as financial worries or depression, may need to be addressed before or at the same time as helping them to support their children as learners.
- Voluntary and community organisations have particular expertise in reaching and engaging vulnerable families, and a proven track record in the kinds of responsive and innovative practices that characterise locally appropriate preventative work (Edwards et al., 2006).

Example from practice
Reaching families who are not using early years services

Redcar and Cleveland has developed a project called 'Play-at-Home'. It involves a series of home visits to children and families with the aim of increasing parent confidence and involvement in their children's play and learning. The families invited to take part are identified as those who are not engaging in other opportunities offered by centres or other local services.

The families receive weekly visits for anything between 6 and 16 weeks. The approach is flexible and adapted to individual needs. Each session lasts for around one hour and usually begins with a rhyme or song, followed by a play activity and then a book or story.

Some parents feel more relaxed at home and take part in playing with their child without feeling self-conscious about playing in front of other parents and professionals. The visits help to build confidence by looking at parents' strengths – the things they do already – as well as the things they would like to change and learn more about.

As the weeks go on, the balance gradually shifts and parents begin to take the lead in playing with their child, with support. Parents are also gradually introduced and encouraged to attend group-based sessions within the Children's Centres and the local community

Source: Wheeler and Connor (2009)

Reviewing services to make them more inclusive

The following checklist can be used to do an 'audit' to establish whether there are relational, practical, contextual, strategic or structural steps that could be taken to make existing services more effective in getting, keeping and engaging parents – both fathers and mothers – or as a planning tool for new services.

Checklist for getting, keeping and engaging parents

	Fully	Could do more
Relationship factors		
Do parents feel welcomed and valued by staff?		
Do practitioners work within an ethos of partnership with and respect for parents?		
If not, are we supporting them to develop their relationship skills?		
Practical factors		
Do we provide adequate childcare facilities?		
Is the service accessible, convenient and welcoming?		
Are services delivered at flexible and convenient times?		
Do parents know about the services?		
Cultural and contextual questions		
Do we take time to find out about personal issues that may affect service uptake, such as financial worries, relationship breakdown, and so on?		
Do we know about issues that could affect a parent's involvement in learning, for example languages spoken at home, literacy, access needs, and so on?		
Do publicity materials and activities make it clear that all parents are welcome, including fathers and parents from different ethnic backgrounds?		
Are services 'father-friendly' in content and style?		

Continued

Continued

Checklist for getting, keeping and engaging parents

	Fully	Could do more
Strategic questions		
Have we consulted parents about service design and activities?		
How well do we know our community?		
Do we make persistent and creative efforts in reaching targeted parents?		
Are practitioners trained and skilled in outreach and family engagement?		
Are there different ways parents can access our service, for example one-to-one home visits as well as joining groups?		
Structural questions		
Are sessions informal and fun with lots of hands-on learning?		
Are there opportunities for parents to share ideas and knowledge with each other?		
Are activities and written information for parents accessible for parents with limited literacy or English as an additional language?		

© Family and Parenting Institute 2009, *Early Home Learning Matters: A good practice guide*

Chapter 4
Models and approaches

In this chapter ...

Whether you're developing services or working directly with parents, this chapter will help you make informed decisions when choosing activities and programmes to support early home learning.

It describes the three essential components of services to extend and enhance parents' knowledge and skills, so that they can create positive home learning environments. Detailed information about a range of resources and programmes to support work with fathers as well as mothers is included.

For practitioners and their managers, this chapter brings together key information about what makes services more effective and the tangible things that practitioners can do to help parents engage confidently in their children's early learning.

What services could be developed or commissioned?

Services to support early home learning are not easy to encapsulate as a specific intervention because of their justified and inevitable overlap with family support services, early years services, parenting support and family learning.

And yet robust and effective services to involve parents, fathers as well as mothers, in providing the kind of interactions and opportunities that have a positive impact on children's learning and development are essential in achieving the best outcomes for children. Therefore, focusing on these outcomes and the factors that help to achieve them needs to be the starting point when making decisions about the types of services to deliver or commission.

Key messages

Services are more effective when they:

- involve parents as well as children

- provide intensive support to vulnerable parents in the first three years to enable them to meet their children's needs

- avoid labelling 'problem families'

- target multiple risk factors

- last long enough to make a difference

- are developed in consultation with parents

- are culturally appropriate.

(Siraj-Blatchford and Siraj-Blatchford, 2009)

In thinking about the kind of services that make up an effective early home learning service, the Harvard Family Research Project (2006) identifies three distinct but overlapping processes.

1. Parenting
   This includes the attitudes and behaviours that underpin positive parenting, including nurturing, warm and responsive parent–child relationships and parental participation in child-centred activities. These are only likely to occur in the context of what Desforges (2003) refers to as "at home good parenting".

2. The relationship between school or early years setting and parent
   This encompasses, for example, practitioner–parent conferences and parents participating in and helping with family events and activities organised by the school or early years setting.

3. Parental involvement in learning activities at home
   This refers to specific educational activities that parents do at home with their children that promote later school success, such as talking, reading, singing rhymes and songs, painting, and so on.

Services that include these three processes are likely to support the elements of early home learning outlined in Figure 4.1 below.

Figure 4.1 **The three elements of services to support early home learning (adapted from Reynolds, 2009)**

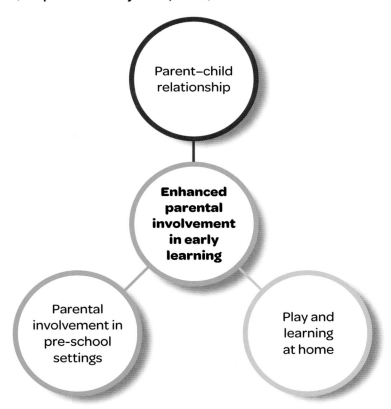

Tailoring services to meet the needs of individual families

"I can see other parents doing things that I want to do differently with my child."
Parent

Interventions to support parental involvement might focus on any or all of the elements in Figure 4.1, but they will not all be necessary for every family. The ELPP showed the importance of practitioners being able to make informed, responsive decisions about the parents' existing strengths and support needs. The following table (also adapted from Reynolds, 2009) illustrates the kinds of interventions that may be appropriate to meet different needs.

Table 4.1 **Implementing the three elements of services to support early home learning**

Processes to enhance parental involvement	Parental involvement in pre-school settings	Playing and learning at home	Parent–child relationship
Parents for whom the intervention may be appropriate	**All settings** need to have in place strategies and initiatives to promote and extend home–setting links. **Some parents** will need extra support to get involved because of personal experiences and attitudes, but most parents are interested and willing to be involved.	**Some parents** will need ideas, encouragement, and resources to create a more stimulating learning environment at home, but are otherwise providing a loving and nurturing parent–child relationship.	**A smaller proportion** of parents will benefit from focused parenting support to help them develop positive parent–child relationships. Some will also need broader parent/family support to help them tackle the issues that make it difficult to parent, e.g. poor mental health, social isolation, poor housing, poverty etc.
Examples of interventions or approaches	• PEAL, PICL and other training for practitioners • Support for transitions to and out of pre-school	• Parents as First Teachers • PEEP • Share	• Family Action Newpin • Family Nurse Partnership (FNP) • Parenting programmes • Parents as First Teachers • Home visiting programmes, e.g. Community Mothers and Home-Start

Putting principles into practice

Supporting parental involvement in pre-school activities

● Effective early childhood settings involve parents in decisions about their child's learning, encourage them to join in activities with their child, and share child-related information between parents and staff (Siraj-Blatchford and Siraj-Blatchford, 2009; Springate et al., 2008; Anning et al., 2007).

- Building strong links between settings and parents is important during transitions into and out of pre-school settings, which can be stressful times for children. This is particularly so for children from minority backgrounds, who may also have to cope with a culture and language that is unfamiliar to them and who are at greater risk of demonstrating poorer behaviour and adjustment on entry to pre-school (Melhuish et al. in Coghlan et al., 2009).

- Evidence from the US on the transition to kindergarten shows that settings that provide opportunities for parent contact, such as home visits, parent discussion groups, parent resource rooms and home lending libraries, notice increased levels of family participation (Ramey et al., 2000).

Practitioner training programmes, such as Parents, Early Years and Learning (PEAL) and Parents Involved in their Children's Learning (PICL), support the development of effective relationships between early years settings and parents. These programmes provide a framework of knowledge, skills, attitudes and resources to facilitate a partnership approach to parental involvement and are described in more detail in Chapter 7.

The early years demonstration projects, ELPP and PPEL, provided opportunities to develop and evaluate innovative practice in involving parents in pre-school activities.

Examples from practice
Parental involvement in pre-school activities

The **Kirklees PPEL** project held a series of Letters and Sounds school picnics for families of children attending the early years settings. The picnics showcased Letters and Sounds activities such as singalongs, a phoneme game and listening diaries.

The **Wakefield Families Enjoying Everything Together (FEET)** project involves practitioners, children and their parents working together on a 10-week course of fun activities designed to enhance language skills during the term before a child enters either pre-school or school.

Getting Ready for Nursery (Nottingham City) is a three-session course on transition issues delivered by Children's Centre practitioners to parents whose children will be moving to school.

Supporting play and learning at home

"I learnt many things. The most important is to find time to play with the boys, taking them to the library and reading, as well as give them attention. I feel more confident now and am going to study for a qualification."
Parent

There are a number of established programmes that have been designed and tested with the aim of increasing parents' knowledge, skills and confidence to play with their child and engage in learning activities at home.

Programmes vary in their focus, but effective interventions to support play and learning at home share common features:

- they happen within the context of a supportive, respectful and affirming relationship between parent and practitioner

- practitioners are able to make informed, responsive decisions about appropriate activities and pace to suit individual parents, and work flexibly to take account of the stresses parents may be facing in their lives

- practitioners or volunteers reflect the cultural or gender profile of the parents with whom they are working

- practitioners use modelling to allow less confident parents to observe practitioners, gain ideas and develop skills at their own pace

- support is offered both in the home and in early years settings, depending on the needs and preferences of the parent.

Enabling parents to make lasting changes and integrate the learning into their daily life as a parent at home may require sustained time and support. This incremental process can be helpfully illustrated using the concept of the 'learning stair'.

Figure 4.2 **The learning stair: helping parents gain confidence and competence in supporting their children's early learning**

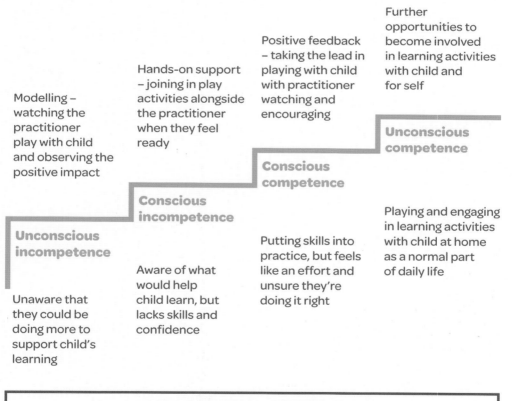

What a parent needs from the practitioner

Further opportunities to become involved in learning activities with child and for self

Positive feedback – taking the lead in playing with child with practitioner watching and encouraging

Hands-on support – joining in play activities alongside the practitioner when they feel ready

Modelling – watching the practitioner play with child and observing the positive impact

Unconscious competence

Conscious competence

Conscious incompetence

Unconscious incompetence

Playing and engaging in learning activities with child at home as a normal part of daily life

Putting skills into practice, but feels like an effort and unsure they're doing it right

Aware of what would help child learn, but lacks skills and confidence

Unaware that they could be doing more to support child's learning

Parent's stage of learning

Existing resources and programmes

There is a huge range of materials to draw from when developing early home learning services. The most effective services use these materials as a starting point and tailor them to local needs and individual families.

Most programmes provide training to practitioners and supporting materials to be delivered by the purchasing organisation; contact details are provided in the Resources section at the end of the book.

Further programmes that focus primarily on training for practitioners are included in Chapter 7.

Resources to promote parental involvement in early learning

Bookstart, Bookstart Plus and Bookstart Treasure Chest

Bookstart is a national programme that aims to encourage parents to share and enjoy books with their children. Bookstart works through health visitors and libraries to give free packs of books to babies and young children, with guidance material for parents and carers.

Positive results have been found in children's pre-literacy (aged 2.5) and literacy (aged 5 and 7), but findings need to be read cautiously given that there were no control groups (Brooks et al., 2008).

Campaign for Learning: Family Learning Works materials

The Family Learning Works programme provides training and materials to enable parents to enjoy learning together as a family. They have worked with parents, particularly fathers, to develop lots of useful tips for parents about becoming their child's 'coach' in order to support their children's early learning.

www.earlyhomelearning.org.uk

A website has been developed to accompany this guide. The website includes a parents' section with information about why parents are so important and what they can do to support their children's learning and development. Practitioners can download this information and print it off to discuss with parents and/or give to parents.

Programmes to promote parental involvement in early learning

I CAN

I CAN is a children's communication charity that works to foster the development of speech, language and communication skills in all children, with a special focus on those who have difficulties with these skills. I CAN provides evidence-based programmes that:

- create communication-friendly settings for children in their early years

- deliver specialist therapy and education for children with the most severe and complex difficulties

- help professionals from across the children's workforce to better support children's communication needs through training and information services

- help parents access the information that they need to support their children.

Family Action Newpin Play Programme

Family Action Newpin Play Programme is aimed at families affected by mental health issues and/or difficulties in the parent–child relationship. Continued evaluation has shown a significant improvement in parents' ability to recognise and meet their children's needs. The programme offers:

- an attachment-based peer support model

- group play and learning opportunities for parent and child over a 12-week period

- a positive experience of playing together for parent and child

- a group experience that is carefully structured to enhance attachment, raise parental self-esteem, and improve the parent's ability to mirror their child's feelings.

Parents as First Teachers

Parents as First Teachers is a home-based parent education and family support programme for families with children pre-birth to five years, which originated in the USA.

Parents as First Teachers provides detailed materials for trained project workers to use when supporting families through structured personal visits. These visits provide:

- regular long-term support to enhance parent–child attachment, on a weekly basis where necessary

- learning through sharing age-appropriate child development information with parents

- help with parenting concerns

- practical support for parents to engage in activities that provide meaningful parent–child interaction and learning opportunities.

Peers Early Education Partnership (PEEP)

The PEEP programme supports parents in developing three particular aspects of learning with their children:

- literacy and numeracy

- self-esteem

- development of learning dispositions.

It has demonstrated a significant impact on the literacy-related skills of children from disadvantaged backgrounds, including gains in children's vocabulary, phonological awareness of rhyme and alliteration, letter identification, and understanding of books, print and writing (Evangelou et al. in Siraj-Blatchford and Siraj-Blatchford, 2009).

The programme uses the four elements of the ORIM (Hannon, 1995) learning framework, which recognises that children need to have:

Opportunities to learn

Recognition and valuing of their early efforts and achievements

Interaction with adults to talk about what they do and how they feel

Modelling by adults of behaviour, attitudes and activities.

The core activities of the programme are:

- songs and rhymes
- sharing books and stories
- activities to encourage parents to talk and play with their child
- talking time – discussion of a theme relating to children's development, giving parents/carers a chance to share experiences together.

Share

Share is a family learning programme developed by ContinYou to help parents support their children's learning at home.

Share materials support the curriculum and are designed to be used by families with children aged 1 to 13 years to share valuable learning time together and have fun. Materials and activities are targeted at literacy, language, numeracy, health and wellbeing.

Supporting the parent–child relationship

"I realised how much I tried to control her and do things for her. Now I know it's important that I encourage her independence – I now try to push her to do things for herself so she realises what she's capable of. I'm more positive and praise her more."
Parent

Most programmes aimed at developing parenting skills have a much broader focus than involvement in children's early learning. Support to improve parenting skills will be a crucial part of work with some parents, however, as the quality of play and learning activities depends on the quality of the parent–child relationship. Recent reviews of interventions to overcome the effects of disadvantage (Coghlan et al., 2009; Springate et al., 2008) and family-based support for early learning (Siraj-Blatchford and Siraj-Blatchford, 2009) have highlighted the role of parenting support programmes in improving social, emotional, behavioural and academic outcomes.

The National Institute for Health and Clinical Excellence's (NICE) *Parent-training/education programmes in the management of children with conduct disorders* (2006) recommended that all parent education programmes, whether group or individual based, should:

- be structured, manual-based and have a curriculum informed by principles of child development theory, and include relationship-enhancing strategies

- offer a sufficient number of sessions, with an optimum of 8–12 sessions

- enable parents to identify their own parenting objectives

- demonstrate proven effectiveness based on evidence from randomised control trials or other suitable rigorous evaluation methods undertaken independently.

There is a range of parenting programmes relevant to the early years (summarised in Table 4.2), which are underpinned by well-established and researched theoretical frameworks.

Table 4.2 Theoretical underpinning of parent education programmes relevant to the early years

Child development theory	Key message	Examples of programmes
Attachment	Forming a strong bond with responsive, sensitive and loving carer(s) is fundamental to successful child development.	• Family Nurse Partnership • Mellow Parenting • Community Mothers • Home-Start • Parents as First Teachers
Social learning	Human behaviour is shaped by its consequences and child behaviour is reinforced by parent response.	• Incredible Years • Triple P • Parents Together
Parenting styles	Children of parents with a warm and authoritative parenting style have higher levels of self-esteem, social responsibility, achievement, mental health and more successful relationships.	• Incredible Years • Triple P • Parents Together
Ecological systems	All children's environments – their homes, schools and communities – need to work together to meet children's developmental needs. Parental involvement in children's education is essential for it to have any lasting impact.	• Strengthening Families, Strengthening Communities • Families and Schools Together

In considering whether to commission or deliver parenting programmes to support the development of positive parent–child relationships, the following factors are relevant.

● Services that integrate parenting, early years and family support services, for instance addressing a child's behaviour and learning difficulties at the same time, result in better outcomes and are more cost effective when working with the most vulnerable families (Hannon et al., 2006; Egeland and Bosquet, 2002; Sanders et al., 2000).

- There is questionable value in delivering programmes that have been designed to address severe behavioural problems to families who do not fall within this group (Scott et al., 2001).

- Home-based interventions to improve parenting skills have been shown to have a positive impact on measures of intellectual development in children. There is also strong evidence to suggest that home visiting can produce positive effects on various dimensions of parenting (Bull et al., 2004).

- The effectiveness of many overseas programmes has been demonstrated by extensive trialling. Programmes developed with a UK population show promising outcomes, but their effectiveness has not yet been tested in the same way.

Examples of home-based and group-based programmes to support the parent–child relationship are shown below. Most programmes provide training to practitioners with supporting materials to be delivered by the purchasing organisation; contact details are provided in the Resources section at the end of this book.

Examples from practice
Home-based parenting programmes

 Community Mothers Programme (CMP) first developed in the UK in 1991 in Thurrock, Essex. It is a preventative initiative that offers disadvantaged parents with young children monthly, home-based support.

Visits are structured, but non-prescriptive, and are based on principles of mutual respect, avoiding dependency and promoting self-help. Parent support groups complement semi-structured home visiting. The model uses a community development approach by recruiting community mothers from the same communities as the parents who are supported.

This intervention has been shown to improve a range of outcomes, including primary immunisations, being read to, more cognitive games, better diet, and less negative and more positive feelings (Johnson et al., 1993). Follow-up found sustained beneficial effects on parenting skills and maternal self-esteem seven years later, with benefits extending to subsequent children, although the trials did not measure the impact on children's cognitive outcomes (Barlow et al., 2007; Sutton et al., 2004).

Other programmes based on the Thurrock model have developed across the UK. Many have close operational links to front-line primary health care and Children's Centre services.

Continued

Continued

 Family Nurse Partnership (FNP), developed in the USA, involves intensive home visits for vulnerable, first time, young parents by trained nurses during pregnancy and the first two years after the child's birth. The programme focuses on improved outcomes across three areas:

- health, wellbeing and improved parenting skills

- enhancing child development and school readiness

- linking the family to wider social networks and employment.

In the USA, large-scale clinical trials have shown the programme to result in significant and consistent improvements in the health and wellbeing of the most disadvantaged children and their families in both the short and long term. Although studies include few measures of children's cognitive attainment, benefits of the programme include:

- improved school readiness

- fewer subsequent pregnancies

- better prenatal health

- reductions of between 50 and 70 per cent in child injuries, neglect and abuse

- increased involvement of fathers.

Source: Utting et al. (2007)

Examples from practice
Group-based parenting programmes

The **Incredible Years** programme has an extensive evidence base that demonstrates a positive impact on parent–child relationships and other aspects of parenting, as well as on parental involvement in schools, school readiness, child social competence, and parent and child problem-solving abilities (see Moran et al., 2004 for a review). Unlike many parenting programmes, its effectiveness and appropriateness have been demonstrated with toddlers and pre-school children.

Parents Together is a flexible programme of workshops and courses varying in length from one to seven sessions, addressing key parenting skills and issues, as well as supporting parents through events such as divorce and separation. The 'early years' series includes:

- relating to babies

- play

- understanding children's behaviour

- helping children learn.

These can be delivered separately or combined together to provide programmes tailored to different needs. Independent programme evaluations have demonstrated:

- increased confidence for both parents and children

- reduced anxiety for both parents and children

- more positive parenting skills

- closer parent–child relationships

- reductions in problem behaviour.

"I now understand more why he behaves that way. I used to just get angry and try to control him. I'm more permissive now and try to be more positive and praise him more."
Parent

Chapter 5
Examples from practice

In this chapter ...

Having looked at the different models, programmes and resources that are available to early years services, this chapter uses real examples from practice to illustrate what works in involving parents in their children's early learning and the key factors for effectiveness.

It provides practical ideas to help practitioners and managers looking for new approaches to strengthen support for early learning at home.

Home visits to encourage play and learning activities at home

"Before the home visitor came, he wouldn't sit down and do things. He'd go off and cry. Now he will sit and read a book. She encouraged him to speak and talked to him as he has language difficulties. I can see now I need to speak to him more about what we're doing, and so on."
Parent

Individual work with families at home is particularly helpful for parents lacking the confidence or inclination to join a group. Practitioners can tailor support to 'where parents are at' in terms of their existing knowledge, skills and confidence, and make informed, responsive decisions about appropriate activities and pace.

Home visits provide regular opportunities to:

- discuss a child's development and learning needs
- support the development of a close and nurturing parent–child relationship
- introduce play and learning activities, such as singing rhymes, playing with dough, painting, and so on
- build a parent's knowledge, confidence and skills through hands-on support and encouragement.

Key factors for effectiveness

- Keep the child the focus of the visit – use the visit as a structured opportunity to model and share play and learning activities with the child, and to discuss them afterwards.

- Visit over a long enough time period to allow the parent to integrate the learning and develop the confidence to play with the child as a normal part of daily life.

- Encourage parents to keep a record of their child's development and learning, so that progress can be discussed during visits to provide motivation, positive feedback and further suggestions. Think about loaning parents a digital camcorder or camera to record their child if they would be more comfortable with a visual rather than written record.

- Be flexible – if a parent is stressed or upset about something else going on in their life when the practitioner arrives, this may need to be tackled first.

Examples from practice

 K has seven children and does not currently have a partner. Her health visitor maintained regular contact with the family and became concerned about the destructive behaviour of her three-year-old, who had a very short concentration span, and the fact that the baby was being kept strapped in his pushchair. She referred the family to Parents as First Teachers.

The Parents as First Teachers worker introduced K to activities to help develop her three-year-old's fine motor skills and games to help encourage gross motor activity. K was worried that her son was walking on his toes and the Parents as First Teachers worker arranged for her to see the health visitor for an assessment, as this may be an early sign of cerebral palsy.

The Parents as First Teachers worker also encouraged K to take the baby out of his chair and lay him on his tummy on the floor. He was not able to sit up, probably because he had spent so much time in a chair. The worker explained that he should be able to sit up unaided and be making attempts to move about, so K dispensed with the chair and followed the worker's advice.

The worker also took books for both children and encouraged K to read and talk with them. K was able to see how playing with and reading to the children helped their development and was motivated to continue.

Source: Family and Parenting Institute (2008)

Continued

M is 20 and is expecting her second child. She lives with her partner. Her health visitor referred her to ELPP because of concerns about her two-year-old daughter, W.

W's language development was delayed, with only five recognisable words, and her attention span was very limited. M's interactions with her daughter included a great deal of negative instruction.

M and the ELPP worker agreed to weekly home visits to support W to extend her vocabulary and to help M manage behaviour through positive reinforcement. The worker was very aware of all the pressures M was dealing with and focused on making the visits fun and relaxing for her, as well as her daughter. Peers Early Education Partnership (PEEP) Learning Together Folders were used to introduce play activities that encouraged talking, singing and looking at books.

The first book left by the ELPP worker was destroyed before the next week's home visit. M was upset by this and explained that she didn't let W have books because she just destroyed them. The worker continued loaning books, suggesting that to begin with M should keep the book for quiet times together.

Weekly home visits were continued for several months due to several major issues within the family – including the birth of a new baby. In addition to the home visits, M was encouraged to take W to a toddler group where she could interact with other children.

The relationship that M built with the ELPP worker also gave her the confidence to join a PEEP group at a local centre run by the same ELPP worker, which she attended regularly, sometimes with her partner.

The double intervention of home visits and participation in a PEEP group was extremely effective for this family. M's knowledge and understanding of her daughter developed, as did her confidence as a parent. She came to recognise real value in W's play and actively offered more play opportunities.

W developed an interest in books and had her own books at home. During one of the later PEEP group sessions, W sat and held a book during 'book time' and turned each page, making comments on the illustrations.

Source: Family and Parenting Institute (2008)

Family play or activity sessions

Group sessions provide opportunities for parents to socialise and get ideas from each other and for children to play with other children. Although setting based, their aim remains to introduce parents and children to play and learning activities that they can do together at home, such as singing, reading books, messy play and number games.

Key factors for effectiveness

- Ensure venues are welcoming, convenient and accessible.

- Use modelling as a core practitioner skill, to allow parents to get ideas from watching staff interact with their child and become more actively involved when they feel ready.

- Provide resources for parents to use at home with their child, for instance books, ideas for creative play, and so on. Bookstart, Storysacks and Treasure Baskets are examples of resources that are available to support early learning activities at home. Contact details are provided in the Resources section at the end of this book.

- Enable parents to set their own learning objectives.

- Provide sessions at different times of the day, including evenings and weekends to include working parents.

- Determine whether childcare may be needed for older or younger children, especially when running groups during evenings and weekends.

Examples from practice

R has clinical depression and struggles to engage with her children most of the time. She had been attending a voluntary sector family service for nine months when she joined a Family Action Newpin Play Programme with her three-year-old son.

Her son was a very angry child and was always telling people to "shut up" and "go away". He struggled to mix with his peers and had limited concentration for activities, as he always wanted to be with R.

R decided her goals were to gain confidence to play with her son; learn new ideas of things she could do with him; feel able to sing with the children and get help with boundaries.

Before they started the programme, all R did was push her son away and tell him to go and play. Initially she was very nervous, but was encouraged by her son's pleasure that she was with him in the playroom, getting involved and giving him positive attention. She enjoyed messy, creative play sessions and helped her son to join in too. During a 'follow your child' activity, R was ill at ease to start with, but got on the floor with her son, doing everything he did and playing as he did.

As the programme continued, her son became more confident and better able to mix with his peers and other adults. He was also more able to separate from R and spend time in the playroom without her. R still struggles at times to play with her son due to her depression, but she now spends time in the playroom with him, is more confident playing with him, understands the importance of play and does more activities with both her children at home.

Source: Family and Parenting Institute (2008)

Dads ACE Project (Coventry) worked with fathers and their children to transform an allotment into an outdoor learning environment. The project focused on developing the dads' and the children's language, literacy, emotional literacy and community skills through growing produce, exploration of the natural environment and child-led learning through play activities.

Source: Department for Children, Schools and Families (2007)

Baby massage classes

"It improved our communication and one-to-one time together. I found new ways to engage with her."
Parent

Baby massage promotes attachment and can improve communication between parents and babies, as well as helping parents find ways of soothing their babies. Small informal groups are run by a qualified instructor to help mothers and fathers learn simple techniques of infant massage.

Key factors for effectiveness

- Keep groups small to allow time for individual attention.

- Recommended age for group classes is from birth to pre-crawling.

- Emphasis should be on enjoying time with the baby and having fun with other parents, as well as learning new skills in a supportive environment.

"You can make it fun and enjoy it – before it used to be stressful, but now I feel more relaxed."
Parent

Example from practice

 Thomas Coram Children's Centre runs regular baby massage courses for parents and babies. An instructor certified by the International Association of Infant Massage runs the sessions over four or five consecutive weeks.

Parents are encouraged to come along and give massage a go – and are reassured that sessions are fun, informal and that it's okay for their baby to cry.

Participants massage their babies while being guided through a step-by-step routine using different massage techniques. Each parent receives individual attention for any special needs and guidance is provided on how massage can be adapted to the growing child. The emphasis is on helping parents to see that they are the experts in their baby by helping them to observe their baby's reactions and what they enjoy and don't enjoy.

"It shows parents that they have the magic touch with their babies and give them what they want. It's a great way for parents to really get to know their babies and follow their cues. Parents who don't feel very confident handling their babies, for instance if their baby was very premature or needed a lot of medical treatment, really benefit."
Thomas Coram Children's Centre practitioner

Parenting support

Encouraging parental involvement in early home learning and parenting support go hand in hand; parents and children playing and joining in learning activities together builds a close and nurturing parent–child relationship, at the same time as promoting cognitive development.

Some parents, however, may need more intensive help with parenting skills to be able to interact positively and play with their children. More focused support for the development of parenting skills may be provided through one-to-one support inside or outside the home or through a group programme.

Key factors for effectiveness

- One size does not fit all. Informed decisions should be made about the specific parenting support needs of the target group and how best to meet these.

- Disadvantaged families have been shown to be the least likely to benefit from group-based parenting programmes either because of problems experienced by the parents and/or because they are the least likely to become, or remain, engaged (Hallam, 2008, cited by Springate et al., 2008).

- A 'stepping stone' approach, combining parenting programmes with more flexible community-based parenting workshops and short courses, has been shown to be more effective in reaching parents whose children are most at risk of poor outcomes and in increasing take-up of longer parenting programmes.

- Providing parents with information in the form of leaflets, DVDs and e-learning, has been found to have beneficial impact and may be one way to reach some parents, although literacy, language or other communication barriers need to be borne in mind (Moran et al., 2004).

"I went along to the parent and toddler play sessions at a local centre. I play more with my child now than I would have done if I hadn't gone. It made me not so worried about messy play. Before I was scared to give him pens or dough because I thought he was too young. He's a lot closer to me now because we do more things together and I understand him more."
Parent

Example from practice

A local authority had been delivering the Incredible Years programme for some time. The impact on parents who attended was positive, but the authority was concerned that the families they really wanted to reach were not participating.

To improve their ability to reach these parents, they trained practitioners across the authority in the Parents Together programme developed by Parentline Plus, a flexible programme of short courses and workshops.

There were initial concerns about the potential for conflicting messages to parents when running two different programmes. These fears proved ungrounded, however, and practitioners found that they were able to blend the approaches that were based on similar theoretical underpinning.

The initial pilot led to a highly positive outcome. Careful monitoring of participants showed that using the Parents Together programme succeeded in reaching more vulnerable families who had not previously accessed support, while take-up of the longer Incredible Years programme also increased.

This combined approach is now used across the authority, with parents able to choose the type of programme that they are comfortable with and that meets their needs, and also progress from one to the other if they wish.

Chapter 6
Meeting the needs of different parents

In this chapter ...

This chapter brings together research and examples from practice to help services reach and engage parents who have traditionally been less likely to access parenting, early learning and family support services.

This chapter will help service providers successfully include fathers, families from different cultures and parents with additional support needs in services to support early learning at home.

The guiding principle in making services accessible to parents in different circumstances is to avoid making assumptions and instead listen to what they say they need. An inclusive approach depends on being proactive in creating and using opportunities to talk to parents with different needs and involve them in the design and implementation of local activities.

"I'm quite logical and need a good reason to do things. I couldn't see the point of doing the same thing over and over again with my baby. Then I joined a dads' group and the worker said 'Well, actually, with repeating this activity, which is probably boring you to tears, you're actually reinforcing the connections in your baby's brain and then it grows . . . because it's like a road and you're reinforcing a road and it stays there, so obviously your child is able to do more things from that. That's really good.' So now I can see the point and know that what I'm doing is actually making a difference and is important."
Parent

Including fathers

Key messages

- Children with fathers involved in their learning do better at school and have better mental health, even after other factors such as father's socio-economic status and education have been taken into account (Flouri and Buchanan, 2001).

- Staff awareness is crucial to involving fathers: embed 'father friendliness' into practitioner training and supervision, and encourage staff to take a proactive approach through discussion at staff meetings, and so on.

- Develop provision and offer activities that appeal to fathers' interests, such as physical activities, and offer services at flexible times.

- Explicitly include fathers in information about children's early learning, using positive language and images.

- Employ male staff in parent contact roles.

Examples from practice

 As part of the ELPP, Action for Children in North Solihull focused their work solely on dads with children between one and three years of age, as this was an under-represented group across local Children's Centres.

They used Parents as First Teachers and Campaign for Learning (CfL) resources to develop different access points for fathers, depending on their needs and confidence. These access points included outreach and social opportunities, such as a photo shoot, a dads' 'stay and play' group, and individual work in the home using Parents as First Teachers materials.

Continued

Continued

The very practical approaches of the CfL Best Coach and Parents as First Teachers materials were effective in keeping fathers involved and offering them something that they were able to take away and use with their children. The development of a website (www.activ-dads.org.uk), which provided links to other sites, was also helpful in engaging fathers and promoting the services of the project.

Source: Family and Parenting Institute (2008)

 Liverpool's Active Play project was based around physical activity for dads and their children aged three to five years who attended targeted Children's Centres and schools.

Active Play workers ran a short course in partnership with the city's Sports, Recreation and Leisure Services to encourage fathers to develop their children's play opportunities using different resources. At the end of the course, fathers were given a rucksack with the equipment they needed to continue to play actively with their children, including a camera, stop watch, whistle and a specially designed fob, giving handy hints for indoor and outdoor games.

Source: Department for Children, Schools and Families (2007)

 The **Me and My Dad** project in Blackburn targeted two communities in deprived wards. This included a community with a high Asian heritage population and one with an indigenous white population. A fathers' worker was appointed, assisted by a part-time Gujarati and Urdu speaking worker.

Fathers were invited to attend weekly sessions in Children's Centres and schools. The Share family learning programme was used as a basis for the activities. Fun activities, such as trips and physical play sessions, were also included.

As part of the project, practitioners' skills and confidence to engage and work with fathers were developed through ContinYou training. This course explored barriers to fathers' involvement in their children's learning and ways of overcoming these barriers.

Source: Department for Children, Schools and Families (2007)

Including parents from black and minority ethnic communities

Key messages

- The link between social disadvantage and children's underachievement affects families from black and minority ethnic communities disproportionately, as they are more likely than other groups to be affected by poverty (Sylva et al., 2004). On top of this, parents whose primary language is not English face additional difficulties in playing a full and active role in their children's education.

- Research provides strong evidence of the benefits of involving black and minority ethnic parents in their children's early learning. The EPPE study (Sylva et al., 2004) found that the effect of the early home learning environment among some black and minority ethnic groups was even stronger than among the white UK group, and had even more influence on children's achievement in literacy and numeracy than would otherwise be expected given their socio-economic status and other circumstances.

- Avoiding assumptions and stereotyping when responding to black and minority ethnic families is crucial. The need to treat each family as unique is backed up by the EPPE research (Sylva et al., 2004), which shows that the variations in parental involvement in early learning were greater within each ethnic group than between groups.

- Services can help to overcome barriers by:
  - ensuring that activities are culturally sensitive
  - employing a staff group whose ethnic diversity reflects the local community
  - encouraging parents to view pre-school provision as promoting educational achievement.

- Involving other parents as key communicators, either in formal roles such as parent champions or through local friendship and peer support groups, is particularly helpful in engaging families from minority ethnic communities.

- Early home learning services should include activities to support parents' language and literacy development, especially where English is not the primary language spoken at home.

- Better monitoring of service take-up among families from black and ethnic minority communities is important in understanding patterns of service use.

Examples from practice

 At Thomas Coram Children's Centre in the London Borough of Camden, one week in the year is designated as Languages Week in order to celebrate the varied home languages spoken by children and families in the community. Over 50 per cent of children speak a language other than English at home.

Parents are invited into the centre to take part in activities – to cook, talk and play, read stories or sing songs and rhymes using their home language. The school library service and a local bookshop are invited to bring resources into the centre, including dual language texts. Many activities are also organised by parents themselves.

The week helps everyone – parents, children and practitioners – to gain more understanding about different languages and cultures. Parents who are uncertain of the importance of maintaining a strong first language, while acquiring English as a second language, are reassured that speaking, playing and reading to children in their home language is a helpful thing to do.

Source: Wheeler and Connor (2009)

 Involving Polish Fathers in Cumbria developed activities to involve fathers from the Polish community. These included computer skills workshops with a play theme for fathers and their children, and residential outdoor pursuits workshops. Literacy and numeracy courses were also provided to enable fathers with low literacy levels to be more involved in their children's education.

Source: Family and Parenting Institute (2008)

Including parents with additional support needs

"How parents experience services early on can really affect how they feel about both services and themselves as mums or dads."
Disabled parent

Parents with additional support needs are a diverse group that includes parents with:

- physical or sensory impairment
- learning disabilities
- mental health needs
- difficulties associated with substance misuse
- long-term medical conditions
- parents who identify as part of the deaf community.

"The Children's Centre's very warm and welcoming. They have sofas and kettles – I can relax and talk freely. It's a break from isolation. It gives me something for myself and my child likes coming. I've learnt things I can do for my child and I've got lots of ideas that I didn't think of myself."
Parent

Key messages

- Parents with additional support needs continue to face difficulties in accessing services that support family life. The separation between children's and adults' services has resulted in a fragmented approach to work with families and different views about whether the focus of support is on child protection or on supporting people with their parenting role (Commission for Social Care Inspection, 2009).

- The ways that services for adults and families are designed, accessed and delivered should ensure that the parenting role is fully supported. The social model of disability, which focuses on what is needed to enable full participation, is helpful in avoiding labelling a disabled parent as a 'problem'. The children of disabled parents should not automatically be seen as children 'in need'. Rather the aim should be to prevent children becoming 'in need' by prioritising services to support adults with their parenting responsibilities (Wates, 2002).

- Parents want support in their own right as individuals and to have their parenting role recognised, without assumptions being made about their parenting capacity. They may be very wary of approaching statutory services, fearing that their parenting will be criticised or undermined. Collaboration between statutory agencies, voluntary sector organisations and community-based projects may be a more successful way of reaching these parents.

- Parents need easy access to support with accessible information and good communication about where to go and what is available, including British Sign Language translation of materials, Easy Read formats and video-phone interpreting.

- Consultation with parents is essential in designing inclusive services and overcoming barriers that individual parents may face in accessing services. One size does not fit all.

- The needs of individual parents should be carefully considered. For instance, deaf parents may need interpreters for practitioner–parent conferences, careful thought may be necessary when organising family 'days out' to ensure that a parent in a wheelchair can take part, and parents with learning difficulties or mental health needs may require intensive one-to-one support to engage in their children's early learning.

B had very recently separated from the mother of his children. He was isolated, a substance user and depressed.

His health visitor visited regularly to find out the kind of support he needed. When B identified that he would like help and ideas to play with his children, aged two and three years, the health visitor brought a worker from the local Children's Centre to meet B and to let him know about the PEEP sessions that were run at the centre.

This initial personal contact in his home enabled B to start attending the PEEP sessions. The sessions involved singing, play activities, such as making flour dough, and storytelling.

Initially B was reluctant to participate, but gradually became more involved as he saw the positive impact on his children. When they first started attending the sessions, his two-year-old son spent all his time with his dummy in his mouth, didn't talk and communicated only with occasional shrieks.

As the weeks passed, he started to talk, mostly repeating two and three syllable words. Although he still used his dummy, he did so less. He took part in singing and action songs and enjoyed story time, especially when he was allowed to turn the pages.

B has now asked for information about a toddler group that he can take the children to.

Source: Family and Parenting Institute (2008)

 C and T both have learning difficulties and sought support in managing their young child's behaviour. Their son, N, was a loud and active child; they were finding it a challenge to keep his attention for any sustained period and he spent his time wandering around the house on his own.

They have family close by, but are otherwise isolated with few friends or community links. Their health visitor was concerned about their parenting capacity and awareness of their son's safety needs, as well as how their learning difficulties could impact on his long-term development. It was felt that they needed support to engage N in age-appropriate play activities.

Continued

A Parents as First Teachers worker started visiting regularly for play sessions in the home to increase the parents' understanding of age-appropriate play and positive interaction with their child. The home visits were also an opportunity to discuss practical behavioural strategies to cope with temper tantrums, and to provide the parents with emotional support and encouragement to build their confidence in looking after N.

T and C were willing to take on board the Parents as First Teachers worker's suggestions and were able to put some of the new ideas into practice. This required lots of repetition and adaptation of the Parents as First Teachers programme to allow for their learning difficulties.

The health visitor also continued to support the family and helped them to access other local family support services, including 'Follow my Child' sessions at the local Children's Centre.

N now has access to a greater range of activities appropriate to his stage of development and mixes with other children. Both parents show greater confidence and are more able to interact with their child in a positive way. As a family, they are accessing more local services and events and making more links with the wider community.

Source: Family and Parenting Institute (2008)

"The worker comes to see me at home and gives me emotional support by talking to me. I don't feel judged and it's given me confidence. She shows me how to use house things as toys and always brings books and toys with her."
Parent

Chapter 7
Managing the work

In this chapter ...

This chapter is aimed at early years managers and commissioners. It will help you develop joined-up services for young families based on a common vision and understanding of the work, and explores the role of Children's Centres as hubs of good practice and multi-agency provision.

The chapter also focuses on the skills, training and continuing professional development needed by the early years workforce to work in partnership with parents and involve them effectively in their children's early learning. Details of available training resources are included.

Lastly, the chapter looks at how to measure the impact of the early home learning services you are developing or providing on outcomes for children.

"Effective practice is characterised by well-integrated services."
(Siraj-Blatchford and Siraj-Blatchford, 2009)

The need for joined-up working has been increasingly highlighted by research, policy guidance and messages from parents, and is reflected in local strategies and plans. Much progress has been made and yet the time, clarity, attitudes and structures needed for successful integration continue to present challenges (Reynolds and Cotton, 2009).

Many of these challenges arise from the diversity of early years provision and confusion about where responsibility for early home learning lies. In some authorities, the lead role is taken by the parenting commissioner; in others, by early years education or extended services; while in others, there is no real strategic lead.

The lack of alignment within early years, with functions split between childcare and education, and the fact that much of the work is provided by the private, voluntary and independent sector, further compound the challenges.

Confusion about which budget early home learning belongs in is also an obstacle to developing provision – in the words of a parenting commissioner:

"Where is the money for parent work, where does it go ... how much in the early years budget should be for parent work, how much in the PCT budget?"

Integrating parenting, early learning, health and family support services

Early home learning services cannot stand alone. They operate within a paradigm of risk versus prevention, and need to be delivered as part of a raft of universal and targeted services to tackle different levels and intensities of difficulties. These may include, for instance, measures to tackle poverty or services for families affected by mental or physical ill health or disability.

In their study of local authority services to support early home learning, Reynolds and Cotton (2009) were able to identify some well-developed and integrated provision. These best practice examples were characterised by:

- strong, clear and enthusiastic leadership at a senior and authority-wide level, combined with committed lead practitioners within Children's Centres

- a 'champion' for the work at operational level who can drive the development of services and pull multi-agency work together

- alignment of education and childcare elements of early years services

- joining up of the early years and parenting agenda

- joined-up working across early years, Children's Centres, education, social care and health

- links with local private, voluntary and independent providers

- supportive frameworks such as authority-wide quality standards, action plans and monitoring and evaluation.

At locality level, Children's Centres can provide an effective hub for joined-up services, hosting initiatives and diverse practitioners, cascading training and good practice, and facilitating links between early years, schools, health and the private, voluntary and independent sectors.

Figure 7.1 The Children's Centre as a hub of joined-up services and activities

Example from practice

Sandwell is a small metropolitan borough that participated in the PPEL project, which ended in 2008.

Strategically, early home learning services sit in Early Years under the Early Years Foundation Stage Phase Leader. The combination of strong leadership and management from the top and committed leadership on the ground to drive forward the PPEL achievements has resulted in integrated working and a healthy partnership between the statutory, private and voluntary sectors.

Delivery is based in Children's Centres, cascading out into local communities. Key elements include:

- a lead practitioner in each Children's Centre who has developed a local action plan for parent involvement, following extensive consultation with parents. Provision to support parent involvement includes:

  o activities focused on play
  o talking to babies and young children
  o baby massage
  o healthy eating
  o free or cheap activities that parents can easily replicate at home.

- a special focus on groups that are not accessing Children's Centre services, such as new arrivals, fathers and working parents. This is achieved through:

  o awareness training for practitioners
  o working in partnership with the Refugee and Asylum Seekers Team
  o information packs and storyboards showing where people have come from
  o joining up with community groups
  o mentoring and buddying for new arrivals
  o football tournament between Children's Centres
  o a Working with Fathers Steering Group
  o weekend activities for working parents.

PEAL training, delivered as part of the PPEL project, is now being rolled out to all settings in the authority, including daycare settings, nurseries and schools. The aim is to have a trainer based in each Children's Centre, so that the training can be continuously rolled out to new staff.

Diverse and evolving roles and skills

"This kind of work calls for an informed workforce, which is able to work responsively within agreed sets of aims to prevent the social exclusion of children and their parents."
(Evangelou et al., 2008)

In the same way that early home learning services defy neat definitions, it can be equally challenging to pin down who is delivering the work.

The development of work with parents over the last few years has led to the emergence of new roles, such as family outreach workers, parent support advisers and early learning mentors working alongside well-established roles such as health visitors. A growth in childminding means that childminders are now one of the largest groups of practitioners providing home-based childcare, play, learning and family support.

There has also been an increase in volunteer roles, such as community mothers and parent buddies, in recognition of the fact that peer-based support is more successful in reaching certain groups of parents.

To add to the complexity of the picture, many within the children's workforce now have parent involvement as part of their role, although their primary expertise lies in work with children.

In considering the training and support needs of this diverse workforce, it is helpful to identify both the tasks involved and the skills that are needed by all practitioners to successfully engage parents in their children's early learning.

Tasks involved in engaging parents in their children's early learning

- Getting to know the local community, what the needs are and where vulnerable families are.

- Outreach to engage the most socially excluded families within the local community, including fathers, those from different cultural backgrounds and parents with additional support needs.

- Consultation, both formal and informal, to involve local parents in the design and implementation of services.

- Fostering and maintaining parents' belief that their children can do well and that they as parents have the ability to support their early learning.

- Building authentic and supportive relationships with parents founded on an understanding and valuing of a parent's role and the home learning environment.

- Understanding the wider family environment of the child.

- Promoting emotional attachment and bonding between parents and children.

- Helping parents to acquire the knowledge, confidence and skills to provide the quality of relationships and learning experiences that their children need.

- Tailoring support to the needs of individual families and to cultural and gender needs.

- Making informed decisions about risk and when specialist services are required.

- Working as part of multi-agency tapestry of service provision.

- Monitoring take-up and evaluating the impact of work with parents on outcomes for children.

Skills needed to engage parents in their children's early learning

Effective practitioners are able to:

- recognise which groups of children are vulnerable to learning delay and undertake creative outreach activities to reach families most in need of support

- listen to and build supportive relationships with parents within an ethos of partnership

- understand why parents and the home learning environment are so important

- engage and work with a wide range of parents, including fathers, parents with different cultural backgrounds and parents with additional support needs

- identify parents' starting points, and make informed and responsive decisions about how to tailor support and resources to the needs of individual families

- engage parents and help them develop the confidence, knowledge and skills to help their children

- help families develop problem-solving skills

- identify difficulties early and know when and how to involve other specialist services

- reflect on their practice

- recognise the potential contributions of partner agencies and work effectively in multi-agency teams.

"It's having an appropriately skilled workforce, to make sure that whatever work they're doing with the parent that they've got the skills to be able to manage it in an effective manner."
Children's Centre coordinator

Training for practitioners

Given the varied professional backgrounds of staff working with parents in the early years, training needs to take account of the different starting points and learning requirements of practitioners.

Workforce development formed a key strand of the ELPP and PPEL project; the programme of work included the offer of PEAL training to participating organisations, as well as programme-specific training. The project was therefore able to generate much useful learning about the training needs of practitioners and ways to meet these, and demonstrated the usefulness of a menu-based approach when developing training plans.

The different elements of training for practitioners can be summarised as in Figure 7.2 below.

Figure 7.2 Key elements of practitioner training to support parent involvement in early learning

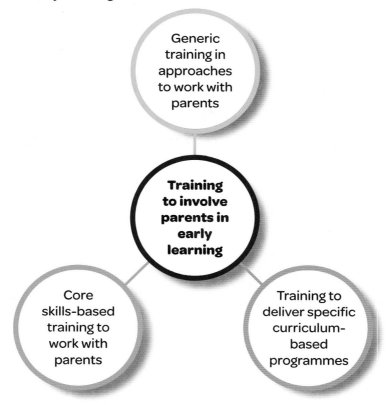

Training programmes

A range of programmes and resources are available to provide training in these three elements. Further information and contact details for a number of providers are included at the end of this book.

Examples of generic training in approaches to work with parents

Parents, Early Years and Learning (PEAL) was developed by the National Children's Bureau (NCB), Coram and the London Borough of Camden. It aims to support practitioners in developing work to engage parents in their children's learning. The programme includes preparatory activities for practitioners to reflect on their current practice, followed by a day's training.

The key elements of the PEAL model are:

● authentic relationships

● communication

● partnership with parents.

The recently published PEAL book, *Parents as partners in the Early Years Foundation Stage – Principles into practice* (Wheeler and Connor, 2009), is listed in the Resources section at the end of the book.

Parents Involved in their Children's Learning (PICL) was developed at Pen Green Centre for Children and their Families in response to the expressed needs of the community. PICL is a way of working that involves respecting the knowledge of parents about their own children, and working with parents in a knowledge-sharing approach.

The PICL Professional Development Programme involves two days' training with the whole staff team in a setting to develop a shared ethos, conduct an audit of current practice and undertake a child study with one family.

A third follow-up training day brings participants together to review and reflect on what they have implemented in their practice since the initial training. By the end of this third day, participants will have developed an action plan for their setting and personal action plans for their own professional development.

One Plus One delivers training in the Brief Encounters® model, which was designed to meet the needs of front-line practitioners working with parents experiencing difficulties in their couple relationship. It is now widely used by practitioners working with a range of family issues within varied contexts. Using the guidelines and boundaries of the training, practitioners gain confidence to:

- listen without becoming overwhelmed
- offer effective support
- encourage clients to seek their own solutions.

Examples of training to deliver specific curriculum-based programmes

Parents as First Teachers: a six-day 'Born to Learn' training prepares practitioners to work with parents of 0- to 3-year-olds. Successful completion is certified by Parents as Teachers International Centre. A two-day follow-on training focuses on work with parents of 3- to 5-year-olds. See Chapter 4 for more information about the programme that practitioners can use with parents, which is provided with the training.

Peers Early Education Partnership (PEEP): PEEP provides a two-day training for practitioners who will be using PEEP materials and ideas within their own work. An optional third day of training leads to accreditation from Oxford Brookes University. See Chapter 4 for more information about the programme that practitioners can use with parents, which is provided with the training.

Share Family Learning Programme: ContinYou trains practitioners over two days, with a half-day follow up, to use the materials with families. See Chapter 4 for more information about the programme that practitioners can use with parents, which is provided with the training.

Examples of core skills-based training to work with parents

Work with Parents is a modular Level 3 qualification within the Qualifications and Credit Framework that maps to the National Occupational Standards. It is accredited by City and Guilds and learners can get an award or a certificate depending on the number of units they undertake.

The **National Academy for Parenting Practitioners** has developed training resources for four of the core modules that can be delivered by local trainers.

The **Training and Development Agency for Schools** offers a training programme for school-based Parent Support Advisers (PSAs), covering local induction, as well as children's workforce modules and PSA role-specific modules. Two vocational Support Work in Schools (SWiS) qualifications at Level 3 offer continuing professional development for PSAs and others with a similar role.

The impact of training on practitioners

Chapter 3 identified poor communication and relationship skills on the part of practitioners as one of the barriers to parental involvement. Training is clearly an important part of tackling this barrier.

Findings from the ELPP project (Evangelou et al., 2008) show that practitioners valued the training they received and that it was vital in changing their attitudes towards parents.

Re-focusing on parents as partners not clients

One of the chief outcomes of the training was a shift in practitioner attitude away from a view of parents primarily as vulnerable clients, and instead seeing them as partners in children's learning. The focus on the primary importance of learning at home and helping parents to enjoy their children also serves to move the focus from 'parents helping teachers' to 'parents as parents' in their own right.

"Before any of the training, I was very nervous about working with parents; I was very much going in to talk to the children and just kind of ignore the parents. But now I'm more confident, and I think because of the training I've received, I've got more knowledge now about how to do it."
Trained teacher who joined a new ELPP team and took part in PEEP and I CAN training

Clear understanding of what to do that helps

Both parents and practitioners in the PPEL project (DCSF, 2008) reported real transformation in the ways in which practitioners communicated with parents about their children's learning. Understanding the research evidence about the importance of the home learning environment and brain development in the early years gives practitioners a clear and common purpose in their work with parents.

"I think perhaps it has made us seize opportunities a bit more, where in the past . . . there might have been opportunities, but as the volunteers hadn't accessed the training, it wasn't at the forefront of our minds as much. I suppose they feel more confident in suggesting something with a family . . . than they would have done before."
Home-Start organiser

Ability to make informed responsive decisions

The dual focus in early home learning services on engaging socially excluded parents at the same time as preparing them to support their children as learners requires practitioners to have the flexibility and skill to respond to different needs and situations.

All training to involve parents in their children's early learning focuses on giving practitioners a set of knowledge, attitudes, skills and resources that they can use flexibly in their work with individual families.

"Their lives are chaotic, hectic and change a lot. You don't know what you're going to be faced with each visit. Each week it can be something else. So

basically if there's something going on that's happened in that week, which is really awful in their life, like rats running across the beds, then they're not going to sit and do sticking and colouring with the children really. But they might sit and read books all together . . . just calming things."
Early years practitioner

"Well we've certainly taken on the PEEP methodology in a big way, but we've adapted it quite considerably in the way that we use the materials and I can quite honestly say that's often on a group-to-group basis. You know what works well for each group."
Early years practitioner

Enthusiasm and motivation

A common theme among practitioners who have undertaken generic training, such as PEAL or programme-specific training, is the sense of 'not being able to wait to put it into practice'. A real thirst for knowledge and understanding was very evident in the ELPP evaluation, regardless of professional background.

"The volunteers love it . . . And some of the volunteers have come back after some of the training and they've gone to see a family and they've come back here so excited about what they've done and what they've achieved."
Early years manager

Making the most of training

Changing the ways in which practitioners interpret their work and providing them with tools and resources to engage parents as effective partners in their children's learning can lead to lasting change in attitudes and ways of working.

The ELPP evaluation showed that there were particular factors that contributed to the successful embedding of training.

Key factors for sustaining the impact of training

- A 'whole setting' approach to training, with every practitioner trained to work in partnership with parents. This integrates parental involvement into every activity and has a much greater impact than specially trained staff delivering discrete programmes to parents.

- Embedding learning through supervision; focused staff meetings to discuss case studies or review progress; and buddying or mentoring by more experienced staff.

- Developing cross-organisational training and practitioner forums to disseminate good practice and ensure a common understanding of, and approach to, early home learning.

- Building parent involvement in children's early learning into the induction training of new staff.

- Recognising and addressing outstanding training needs that may be impeding service development, such as training in outreach, multi-agency teamwork or project management.

"The really crucial bit is buddying them up with a setting where their practice is more advanced, going out and having a look and discussing with practitioners who are doing it."
Head of early years

Evaluating the impact of the work

How will you know whether the services you are providing to support early home learning are making a difference to children's achievement and wellbeing?

Effective monitoring and evaluation is a crucial and integral part of service development, enabling services to:

- assess the effectiveness of current activities and plan future service development

- disseminate knowledge about what works

- justify future investment in early home learning.

Local project evaluation needs to be underpinned by an authority-wide approach to monitoring and evaluation to identify key outcomes and develop a common framework for the collection and analysis of data. This is essential in enabling a robust assessment of the impact of work with parents on long-term outcomes for children.

The following planning and evaluation cycle (Figure 7.3) shows how outcomes and measures need to be built into service planning and development from the beginning.

Figure 7.3 Planning and evaluation cycle

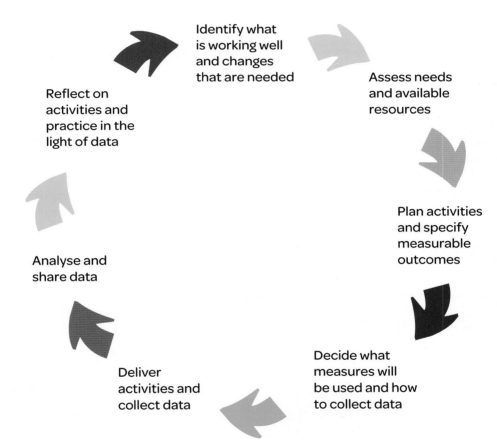

Identify what is working well and changes that are needed

Assess needs and available resources

Reflect on activities and practice in the light of data

Plan activities and specify measurable outcomes

Analyse and share data

Decide what measures will be used and how to collect data

Deliver activities and collect data

Defining outcomes

Outcomes describe what will have changed for children as well as their parents as a result of a service intervention or activity. Examples of outcomes of activities to support early home learning could be that a child will achieve age-appropriate levels of pre-literacy or that a parent will feel more confident in playing with their child.

Outcomes are separate from outputs, which describe what the service will do to achieve the outcomes, for instance deliver weekly home visits.

In deciding on outcomes, careful consideration needs to be given to:

- baseline data, i.e. what is the current situation and what need does the data show that will be addressed by the intervention?

- the specific aim of the intervention, i.e. what change are you planning to make to the baseline data?

- long-term and short-term outcomes, for example what changes are you hoping to make to a child's language skills by the end of a three-month home visiting intervention, and what changes do you hope the service will make to their cognitive development by the time they start school?

- making sure outcomes are specific, measurable, achievable, realistic and timed (SMART).

Designing monitoring and evaluation processes

"Not more forms!" can be a common reaction from both parents and practitioners when presented with an evaluation questionnaire. And yet, when used sensitively and appropriately, monitoring and evaluation processes can provide parents and practitioners with encouraging feedback and increased confidence, as well as ensuring that resources and services really make a difference for children.

How monitoring and evaluation is carried out is what makes a difference, in terms of both the data that it generates and its usefulness to parents' and practitioners' learning.

Good practice guidelines for collecting data

- Monitoring and evaluation tools are parent, child and practitioner friendly.

- Data collection methods are 'fit for purpose' and sustainable: they don't collect more information than is necessary, and contribute to a valuable learning experience for both parents and practitioners.

- Innovative and varied data collection methods are used to include parents with different literacy and linguistic needs, for instance video diaries.

- Both qualitative and quantitative evidence is included. Information is collected about the effectiveness of the processes used in work with parents, as well as about the outcomes.

- Evaluation processes enable comparison and continuous tracking against baseline data to demonstrate impact, for example the use of pre- and post-normative questionnaires.

- Evaluation methods combine locally developed processes with standardised external analytical tools.

- Practitioners are trained to use evaluation tools effectively and to encourage parent participation in evaluation by explaining the purpose and benefits, and providing necessary support.

- Information is shared with parents (at an individual and service level) and practitioners to support reflection, confidence-building and learning.

There are a number of sources of specialist advice that can provide more information about standard measures you can use to evaluate your service, and that can help you to design an evaluation process that meets your needs. These include:

- the research department within your authority

- research departments within university schools of social care or psychology

- National Academy for Parenting Practitioners research team

- Family and Parenting Institute

- independent research consultants.

Chapter 8
Next steps

In this chapter . . .

This chapter is for anyone involved in planning or developing work with parents in the early years and brings together the contents of the previous chapters.

It will help you put the theory into practice by providing a checklist of the key steps involved in developing effective and high-quality services to support early learning at home.

The checklist directs you to the relevant chapters of this book or external resources for more information on each step.

Checklist for developing services or extending what you already offer

Checklist for service development	Key considerations and more information
What services are you already providing to involve parents in early home learning?	Chapter 4 describes the kind of services that support early home learning to help you carry out an audit of existing services.
Do these services include work with parents in the home?	Consider whether including home-based services would enable you to include vulnerable parents more effectively (see Chapters 3, 4 and 5).
How will you consult parents about the kind of services they need and involve them in developing the service?	Parent forums or steering groups can enable parents to have a voice in shaping services. Consider whether training may be needed for these parents to play an active role. The Family Policy Alliance have produced a Parent Participation toolkit that will help you ensure effective parent involvement and consultation (www.frg.org.uk/reports_parent_participation.html).
Who are you targeting?	Consider the key risk factors for children in terms of learning delay (see Chapter 3) and identify local areas of need as well as vulnerable families within these areas.
How are you going to reach them?	Identify the barriers to engagement and ways of overcoming them (see Chapter 3).
How will you reach and engage under-represented groups, such as fathers, parents from minority ethnic communities and parents with additional support needs?	One size doesn't fit all. See Chapters 3 and 6 for information about tailoring outreach and services to include parents with different needs.
How do you want to develop existing services?	Services adopting a multi-component approach have been shown to be most effective. Which services will be universal and which will be targeted? Chapter 4 gives an overview of different models and approaches you could use.
Are there existing programmes to involve parents in their children's early learning that would meet local needs?	See Chapter 4 for more information about available programmes and resources.
Will you deliver the services internally or will you put the services out to tender?	Consider the strength of the private and voluntary sector in reaching and engaging vulnerable families (see Chapter 3).
Will additional funding be needed, and if so, where will it come from?	Sustainable funding for long-term investment in prevention is crucial in making a real impact on outcomes for children.
What outcomes are you trying to achieve?	Outcomes for children should be at the heart of early home learning services. Chapter 1 presents messages from research about the importance of the early home learning environment in improving outcomes for children.

Continued

Continued

Checklist for developing services or extending what you already offer

Checklist for service development	Key considerations and more information
How will you achieve these outcomes?	Consider the key issues that influence the effectiveness of early home learning services outlined in Chapter 4.
How will you monitor and evaluate the service?	Think about how you will know the service is making a difference (see Chapter 7).
Where will the service be based?	Consider a mixed economy of services and settings to reach and engage vulnerable parents (see Chapter 4).
What is your desired timescale for development of the service?	Consider the time needed to identify and reach your target group (see Chapter 3) and the need to train staff (see Chapter 7).
Which departments and agencies need to be consulted and involved?	Consider the need for integrated and joined-up working between health visiting, early years, parenting support, family support services and school improvement (see Chapter 7).
Who can provide advice to help you plan this service?	There is already a body of expertise and experience in what works in parent involvement in the early years. Contact your local National Strategies Early Years Adviser or look at the Resources section at the end of this book for other sources of information.
Who will deliver it?	Consider the capacity of existing staff resources and/or whether additional recruitment will be needed. Chapter 7 addresses the workforce implications of an early home learning service.
What training will these staff need?	Consider the need for training in outreach skills as well as the actual work of involving parents in their children's play and learning (see Chapter 7).
Which existing training programmes could meet local staff development needs?	See Chapter 7 for more information about available practitioner training programmes.
How will staff be supported and supervised?	Consider the supervision needs of staff working with vulnerable parents, particularly when working in parents' homes (see Chapter 7).
What continuous professional development arrangements will you put in place?	Chapter 7 highlights the importance of ongoing staff development in ensuring best practice and service outcomes.

Resources

Information and support

Resource	Support and information provided	Contact details
Early Home Learning Matters	Accompanying website to this guide. Contains a parents' section with resources to download and share with parents.	www.earlyhomelearning.org.uk
National Strategies	Information and resources to support the development of effective practice with children and parents in early years settings.	www.nationalstrategies.standards.dcsf.gov.uk/earlyyears/eyfs
Together for Children	Works in partnership with the Department for Children, Schools and Families to support local authorities in their delivery of Sure Start Children's Centres.	www.childrens-centres.org www.togetherforchildren.co.uk
Family and Parenting Institute	Researches what matters to families and disseminates information to support good practice.	www.familyandparenting.org 020 7424 3460
Centre for Excellence and Outcomes in Children and Young People's Services	Brings together 'what works' to support local authorities and children's trusts to improve outcomes for children, young people and their families.	www.c4eo.org.uk 020 7843 6358
Family Policy Alliance	Informative and practical toolkit for consulting and involving parents in service design and implementation.	www.frg.org.uk/reports_parent_participation.html
Fatherhood Institute	Information, resources, consultancy and training on engaging fathers in early years services.	www.fatherhoodinstitute.org
Parentline Plus	Website includes resources for parents and practitioners, free helpline for parents and training for practitioners.	www.parentlineplus.org.uk 020 7284 5500

Continued

Continued

Resource	Support and information provided	Contact details
Pre-School Learning Alliance	Support and information for early years education and work with parents as partners.	www.pre-school.org.uk 020 7697 2500
National Childminding Association	Promotes and supports childminding expertise and high-quality home-based childcare, play, learning and family support.	www.ncma.org.uk 0800 169 4486

Books and resources

Resource	Information provided	Further details
Why love matters: how affection shapes a baby's brain (2004), Sue Gerhardt, Routledge	An accessible and informative book about the importance of attachment and interaction on early brain development.	www.whylovematters.com ISBN 978-1-58391-817-3
What every parent needs to know: the incredible effects of love, nurture and play on your child's development (2007), Margot Sunderland, Dorling Kindersley NB This book was previously called *The science of parenting*. The content is unchanged.	An illustrated easy-to-read book for parents about how to give their children what they need, with information about parenting linked to early brain development.	ISBN 978-1-40532-036-8
Parents as partners in the Early Learning Foundation Stage – Principles into practice (2009), Helen Wheeler and Joyce Connor, National Children's Bureau	A practical resource for early years settings based on the work of PEAL.	www.ncb.org.uk ISBN 978-1-905818-43-3 Book sales 0845 458 9910
How helping works: towards a shared model of process (2006), Dorit Braun, Hilton Davis and Penny Mansfield	Short and accessible guide for practitioners that provides a practical framework for working in partnership with parents.	Can be downloaded at www.parentlineplusforprofessionals .org.uk/cmsFiles/policy_briefings/ How-helping-works021106.pdf

Continued

Continued

Resource	Information provided	Further details
National Literacy Trust	Information and downloadable resources to support parents to interact with their babies, including information about baby massage.	www.literacytrust.org.uk/talktoyour baby
Campaign for Learning	Resources for family learning developed in partnership with parents, including fathers.	www.campaign-for-learning.org.uk 020 7930 1111
Bookstart	Free packs of books for babies, toddlers and young children available via health visitors, Children's Centres and libraries.	www.bookstart.org.uk 020 8516 2977
Storysacks	Cloth bags containing resources to encourage children and adults to enjoy reading together.	www.storysack.com
Treasure Baskets	Resources provided as part of PEEP programme – see below.	www.peep.org.uk 01865 397970
Change4Life	Practical information and resources for parents about diet and exercise.	www.nhs.uk/change4life

Generic practitioner training

Organisation	Type of training	Contact details
National Children's Bureau	PEAL training and framework for early years practitioners.	www.ncb.org.uk www.peal.org.uk 020 7843 6000
Pen Green Centre for Children and Families	PICL training and framework for early years practitioners.	www.pengreen.org 01536 443435
National Academy for Parenting Practitioners	Training for practitioners in core skills for work with parents and evidence-based parenting programmes.	www.parentingacademy.org 020 7848 7500
Training and Development Agency for Schools	Training for Parent Support Advisers and others in similar roles.	www.tda.gov.uk 020 7023 8000
Children's Workforce Development Council	Training and qualifications for the Early Years Foundation Stage.	www.cwdcouncil.org.uk/early-years 0113 244 6311

Continued

Continued

Organisation	Type of training	Contact details
One Plus One	Training and resources for practitioners on Brief Encounters® model for work with parents experiencing couple relationship problems.	www.oneplusone.org.uk 020 7553 9530

Programme-specific training and materials

Programme	Training and materials provided	Contact details
I CAN	Programme and practitioner training to support development of children's speech, language and communication skills.	www.ican.org.uk 0845 225 4071
Family Action Newpin Play Programme	Programme to support attachment and play in families where there are mental health issues or difficulties in the parent–child relationship.	www.family-action.org.uk 020 7254 6251
Parents as First Teachers	Structured programme and practitioner training to promote attachment and early learning delivered largely in the home.	www.parentsasfirstteachers.org.uk 01844 345847
Peers Early Education Partnership (PEEP)	Structured programme and practitioner training to promote parent involvement in early learning delivered largely in settings.	www.peep.org.uk 01865 397970
Share	Family learning materials and practitioner training developed by ContinYou.	www.continyou.org.uk 024 7658 8440
Thurrock Community Mothers Programme	Early years home support programme provided by trained volunteers.	01375 858512
Home-Start	Early years home support programme provided by trained volunteers.	www.home-start.org.uk 0114 278 8988
Incredible Years	Webster-Stratton parenting programme designed for parents of young children.	www.incredibleyears.com www.parentingacademy.org
Parents Together	Practitioner training and modular group-based parenting programme that can be used flexibly to meet the needs of different parents.	www.parentlineplus.org.uk 020 7284 5500

Glossary

Early years research studies have often commented on the need for clarity about what is meant by words such as 'involvement', 'engagement' and 'at risk'. This glossary sets out the meanings that are used in this book.

Children at risk of learning delay: children who are falling behind in terms of intellectual, emotional and personal development. The term 'learning delay' is not used here as a clinical diagnosis or assessment of special educational needs.

Early home learning: everything that children do or experience at home that influences their learning, development and later achievement.

Early home learning environment: the kind of relationships and opportunities that children experience where they live.

Engaging parents: the process of enabling parents to take up the help that is on offer or access early learning facilities and activities.

Parents: anyone involved in bringing up children, including fathers, mothers, grandparents, step-parents, other family members and carers.

Parent involvement: this term is used to describe the goal of work with parents in the early years – the ongoing active participation of parents in children's early learning as part of daily family life at home.

Practitioner: anyone working with parents in the early years, including childminders, Children's Centre workers, health visitors, teachers and voluntary and private sector workers.

Reaching parents: the first stage of initial communication and making contact with parents.

Setting: a centre or venue where activities for young children and their parents are provided.

Vulnerable families: families with one or more factors that research has shown to be linked to poor outcomes and underachievement in children. These factors are described in Chapter 3.

Abbreviations

Abbreviations are written in full the first time they appear in the book. More information about the programmes and projects listed is provided in the Resources section (page 91).

C4EO	Centre for Excellence and Outcomes in Children's and Young People's Services
CfL	Campaign for Learning
CMP	Community Mothers Programme
CWDC	Children's Workforce Development Council
DCSF	Department for Children, Schools and Families
ELPP	Early Learning Partnerships Project 2006–08
EPPE	Effective Provision of Pre-School Education study
EYFS	Early Years Foundation Stage
FNP	Family Nurse Partnership
FPI	Family and Parenting Institute
NAPP	National Academy for Parenting Practitioners
NCB	National Children's Bureau
NESS	National Evaluation of Sure Start
NICE	National Institute for Health and Clinical Excellence
PEAL	Parents, Early Years and Learning
PEEP	Peers Early Education Partnership
PICL	Parents Involved in their Children's Learning
PPEL	Parents as Partners in Early Learning project 2006–08
PSA	Parent Support Adviser
SSLP	Sure Start Local Programme
SWiS	Support Work in Schools qualification
TDA	Training and Development Agency for Schools

References

Ainsworth, M.D.S., Bell, S.M. and Stayton, D.J. (1971) Individual differences in strange situation behaviour of one-year-olds. In H.R. Schaffer (Ed.), *The origins of human social relations*. London: Academic Press.

Anning, A. and National Evaluation of Sure Start (NESS) Team (2007) *Understanding variations in effectiveness amongst Sure Start Local Programmes: lessons for Sure Start Children's Centres*. London: Department for Children, Schools and Families.

Asmussen, K. (2009) *What is evidence-based practice?* National Academy for Parenting Practitioners briefing paper. Online at www.parentingacademy.org/training_ebpractice.aspx (accessed May 2009).

Barlow, J., Kirkpatrick, S., Wood, D. and Stewart-Brown, S. (2007) *Family and parenting support in Sure Start Local Programmes*. London: Department for Children, Schools and Families (reference: NESS/2007/SF/023). Online at www.dcsf.gov.uk/research/data/uploadfiles/NESS2007SF023.pdf (accessed April 2009).

Barnet and Barnet (1998) quoted in Department for Education and Skills (2003) *Young brains*. London: Department for Education and Skills (report number: 444 P118).

Belsky, J., Barnes, J., and Melhuish, E. (Eds.) (2007) *The National Evaluation of Sure Start: does area-based early intervention work?* Bristol: The Policy Press.

Bowlby, J. (1988) *A secure base: parent–child attachment and healthy human development*. New York: Basic Books.

Bradley, R.H., Corwyn, R.F., Burchinal, M., Pipes-McAdoo, H. and Garcia-Coll, H. (2001) The home environments of children in the United States Part II: Relational with behavioural development through age thirteen. *Child Development*, **72(6)**, 868–1886.

Braun, D., Davis, H. and Mansfield, P. (2006) *How helping works: towards a shared model of process*. London: Parentline Plus/Centre for Parent and Child Support/One Plus One.

Brooks, G., Pahl, K., Pollard, A. and Rees, F. (2008) *Effective and inclusive practices in family literacy, language and numeracy: a review of programmes and practice in the UK and internationally*. Reading: CFBT Education Trust.

Bull, J., McCormick, G., Swann, C. and Mulvihill, C. (2004) *Ante- and post-natal home-visiting programmes: a review of reviews. Evidence briefing summary*. London: Health Development Agency. Online at www.nice.org.uk/nicemedia/documents/home_visiting_summary.pdf (accessed April 2009).

Centre for Excellence and Outcomes in Children and Young People's Services (2009) *Progress map – narrowing the gap in outcomes for young children through effective practice in the early years*. Online at www.c4eo.org.uk/themes/earlyyears/ntg (accessed April 2009).

Coghlan, M., Bergeron, C., White, K., Sharp, C., Morris, M. and Rutt, S. (2009) *Narrowing the gap in outcomes for young children through effective practices in the early years*. London: Centre for Excellence and Outcomes in Children and Young People's Services.

Commission for Social Care Inspection (2009) *Supporting disabled parents: a family or a fragmented approach?* Newcastle: Commission for Social Care Inspection. Online at www.cqc.org.uk/_db/_documents/Dis_parents6.pdf (accessed April 2009).

Department for Children, Schools and Families (2008) *Parents as Partners in Early Learning (PPEL) project: final report 2008.* London: Department for Children, Schools and Families.

Department for Children, Schools and Families/Family and Parenting Institute (2008) *Supporting parents to engage in their child's early learning.* London: Family and Parenting Institute. Online at www.familyandparenting.org/item/document/1727/1 (accessed April 2009).

Department for Children, Schools and Families (2007) *Parents as Partners in Early Learning (PPEL) Project. Parental involvement – a snapshot of policy and practice.* PPEL project phase 1 report. Online at www.surestart.gov.uk/_doc/P0002435.PDF (accessed April 2009).

Department for Children, Schools and Families (2007) *The Children's Plan: building brighter futures.* London: The Stationery Office.

Department for Education and Skills (2002) *Birth to Three Matters: a framework to support children in their earliest years, literature review.* London: Department for Education and Skills.

Desforges, C. with Abouchaar, A. (2003) *The impact of parental involvement, parental support and family education on pupil achievements and adjustments: a literature review.* London: Department for Education and Skills (research report number: 433).

Edwards, A., Barnes, M., Plewis, I. and Morris, K. (2006) *Working to prevent the social exclusion of children and young people: final lessons from the National Evaluation of the Children's Fund.* Birmingham: National Evaluation of the Children's Fund.

Egeland, B. and Bosquet, M. (2002) Emotion regulation in early childhood: the role of attachment-oriented interventions. In Zuckerman, E.B., Lieberman, A. and Fox, N. (Eds.), *Socioemotional regulations: dimensions, development trends and influences.* Skillman, NJ: Johnson and Johnson Paediatric Institute.

Evangelou, M., Sylva, K., Edwards, A. and Smith, T. (2008) *Supporting parents in promoting early learning: Early Learning Partnerships Project.* London: Department for Children, Schools and Families (reference number: DCSF-RR039/DCSF-RB039). Online at www.dcsf.gov.uk/rsgateway/DB/RRP/u015140/index.shtml (accessed April 2009).

Family and Parenting Institute (2008) *Early Learning Partnerships Project (ELPP): Summary.* London: Family and Parenting Institute. Online at www.familyandparenting.org/ELPP (accessed April 2009).

Feinstein, L. (2003) *Very early evidence: how early can we predict future educational achievement?* London: CentrePiece, London School of Economic and Political Science. Online at http://cep.lse.ac.uk/centrepiece/v08i2/feinstein.pdf (accessed April 2009).

Flouri, E. and Buchanan, A. (2001) Father time. *Community Care*, October, **40**, 4–10.

Gutman, L.M. and Feinstein L. (2007) *Parenting behaviours and children's development from infancy to early childhood: changes, continuities and contributions.* London: Wider Benefits of Learning (research report number: 22).

Hannon, P. (1995) *Literacy, home and school: research and practice in teaching literacy with parents.* London: Falmer Press.

Hannon, P., Morgan, A. and Nutbrown, C. (2006) Parents' experiences of a family literacy programme. *Journal of Early Childhood Research*, **3**, 3.

Hart, B. and Risley, T. (1995) *Meaningful differences in everyday parenting and intellectual development in young American children.* Baltimore: Brookes. Online at www.literacyfree.com/research/research3.php (accessed April 2009).

Harvard Family Research Project (2006) *Family involvement makes a difference in school success.* Online at www.hfrp.org/publications-resources/browse-our-publications/family-involvement-makes-a-difference-in-school-success (accessed April 2009).

Hobcraft, J. (1998) *Childhood experiences and the risks of social exclusion in adulthood.* London: London School of Economics STICERD (research paper number: CASEBRIEF08). Online at www.ssrn.com/abstract=1163091.

Johnson, Z., Howell, F. and Molloy, B. (1993) Community Mothers' Programme: a randomised controlled trial of non-professional intervention in parenting. *British Medical Journal,* **306**, 1449–52. Online at www.pubmedcentral.nih.gov/picrender.fcgi?artid=1677859&blobtype=pdf (accessed April 2009).

Lyons et al. (2000) in Gerhardt, S. (2004) *Why love matters: how affection shapes a baby's brain.* Oxford: Routledge.

Melhuish, E. et al. (2001) in Coghlan, M., Bergeron, C., White, K., Sharp, C., Morris, M. and Rutt, S. (2009) *Narrowing the gap in outcomes for young children through effective practices in the early years.* London: Centre for Excellence and Outcomes in Children and Young People's Services.

Moran, P., Ghate, D. and Van der Merwe, A. (2004) *What works in parenting support? A review of the international evidence.* London: Department for Education and Skills (research report number: RR574). Online at www.prb.org.uk/wwiparenting/RR574.pdf

National Institute for Health and Clinical Excellence (2006) *Parent-training/education programmes in the management of children with conduct disorders.* London: National Institute for Health and Clinical Excellence with Social Care Institute for Excellence.

National Literacy Trust (2001) *Parental involvement and literacy achievement: the research evidence and the way forward. A review of the literature prepared by the National Literacy Trust.* Consultation paper. London: National Literacy Trust.

Nutbrown, C., Hannon, P. and Morgan, A. (2005) *Early literacy work with families.* London: Sage Publications.

O'Connor, T.G. and Scott, S.B.C. (2007) *Parenting and outcomes for children.* London: Joseph Rowntree Foundation/King's College London. Online at www.jrf.org.uk/sites/files/jrf/parenting-outcomes.pdf (accessed April 2009).

Olds, D.L. (2006) The Nurse Family Partnership: an evidence-based preventive intervention. *Infant Mental Health Journal,* **27(1)**, 5–25.

Perry, B.D. (2005) *The power of early childhood.* Texas: ChildTrauma Academy/Kansas: Kansas Health Foundation 2005 Leadership Institute. Online at www.slc.edu/media/cdi/pdf/Longfellow08_Perry_Policy.pdf

Peters, M., Seeds, K., Goldstein, A. and Coleman, N. (2007) *Parental involvement in children's education survey.* London: Department for Children, Schools and Families (report number: 034).

Quinton, D. (2004) *Supporting parents: messages from research.* London: Jessica Kingsley Publishers.

Ramey, S.L., Ramey, C.T., Philips, M.M., Lanzi, R.G., Brezausek, C., Katholi, C.R., Snyder, S. and Lawrence, F. (2000) *Head start children's entry into public school. A report on the national head start/public early childhood transition demonstration study.* Washington: Administration on Children, Youth and Families.

Reynolds, J. (2009) *Supporting the early home learning environment: a review of the literature.* Unpublished.

Reynolds, J. and Cotton, D. (2009) *Supporting the early learning home environment: messages from research with local authorities and insights from literature.* Unpublished.

Sanders, M.R., Montgomery, D. and Brechman-Toussaint, M. (2000) The mass media and the prevention of child behaviour problems: the evaluation of a television series to promote outcomes for parents and their children. *Journal of child psychology and psychiatry*, **41(7)**, 939–48.

Schore (1994) in Gerhardt, S. (2004) *Why love matters: how affection shapes a baby's brain*. Oxford: Routledge.

Scott, S., Spender, Q., Doolan, M. Jacobs, B. and Aspland, H. (2001) Multicentre controlled trial of parenting groups for childhood antisocial behaviour in clinical practice. *British Medical Journal*, **323**, 191–94.

Sidebotham, P., Heron, J. and Golding, J. (2002) Child maltreatment in the 'Children of the Nineties': deprivation, class and social networks in child abuse and neglect. *Child Abuse and Neglect*, **26(12)**, 1243–59.

Siraj-Blatchford, I. and Siraj-Blatchford, J. (2009) *Improving children's attainment through a better quality of family-based support for early learning*. London: Centre for Excellence and Outcomes in Children and Young People's Services (C4EO).

Siraj-Blatchford, I. and McCallum, B. (2005) *An evaluation of Share at the Foundation Stage: final evaluation report*. London: Institute of Education.

Siraj-Blatchford, I., Sylva, K., Muttock, S., Gilden, R. and Bell, D. (2002) *Researching effective pedagogy in the early years*. London: Department for Education and Skills.

Snow, C.E., Burns, M.S. and Griffin, P. (1998) *Preventing reading difficulties in young children*. Washington DC: National Academy Press.

Springate. I., Atkinson, M., Straw, S., Lamont, E. and Grayson, H. (2008) *Narrowing the gap in outcomes: early years (0–5)*. Slough: NFER.

Sroufe, L.A., Egland, B., Carlson, E.A. and Collins, W.A. (2005) *The development of the person: the Minnesota study of risk and adaptation from birth to adulthood*. New York: Guilford.

Sutton, C., Utting, D. and Farrington, D. (Eds.) (2004) *Support from the start: working with young children and their families to reduce the risks of crime and anti-social behaviour*. London: Department for Education and Skills (research report number: 52).

Sylva, K., Melhuish, E., Sammons, P., Siraj-Blatchford, I. and Taggart, B. (2004) *The Effective Provision of Pre-School Education (EPPE) project: final report. A longitudinal evaluation 1997–2004*. London: Department for Education and Skills.

Utting, D., Monteiro, H. and Ghate, D. (2007) *Interventions for children at risk of developing antisocial personality disorder*. London: Policy Research Bureau.

Wates, M. (2002) *Supporting disabled adults in their parenting role*. York: Joseph Rowntree Foundation. Online at www.jrf.org.uk/publications/supporting-disabled-adults-their-parenting-role (accessed April 2009).

Whalley, M. (2001) *Involving parents in their children's early learning*. London: Paul Chapman Publishing.

Wheeler, H. and Connor, J. (2009) *Parents, early years and learning. Parents as partners in the Early Years Foundation Stage – Principles into practice*. London: National Children's Bureau.

Index